I Believe I'll Testify

Other books by Cleophus J. LaRue
from Westminster John Knox Press

The Heart of Black Preaching

*More Power in the Pulpit: How America's Most Effective Black
Preachers Prepare Their Sermons*

*Power in the Pulpit: How America's Most Effective Black
Preachers Prepare Their Sermons*

*This Is My Story: Testimonies and Sermons of Black Women
in Ministry*

I Believe I'll Testify

The Art of African American Preaching

Cleophus J. LaRue

WESTMINSTER
JOHN KNOX PRESS
LOUISVILLE • KENTUCKY

First edition
Published by Westminster John Knox Press
Louisville, Kentucky

11 12 13 14 15 16 17 18 19 20—10 9 8 7 6 5 4 3 2 1

Book design by Sharon Adams
Cover design by Lisa Buckley
Cover photograph: © Paul Burns/Getty Images

Library of Congress Cataloging-in-Publication Data

LaRue, Cleophus James
    I believe I'll testify : the art of African American preaching / Cleophus J. LaRue.
        p. cm.
    ISBN 978-0-664-23677-9 (alk. paper)
    1. African American preaching. I. Title.
    BV4221.L37 2011
    251.0089'96073—dc22

                                                                    2010036831

PRINTED IN THE UNITED STATES OF AMERICA

∞ The paper used in this publication meets the minimum requirements of the
American National Standard for Information Sciences—Permanence of
Paper for Printed Library Materials, ANSI Z39.48-1992

Westminster John Knox Press advocates the responsible use of our natural resources.
The text paper of this book is made from 30% post-consumer waste.

For my parents,
Tommie Letha Rice LaRue
and
Cleophus LaRue Sr.
(1924–2008)

While I Have a Chance

I believe I'll testify
while I have a chance.
I believe I'll testify
while I have a chance.
I believe I'll testify
while I have a chance,
for I may not, may not have this chance again.

James Cleveland

Contents

Preface

As a boy growing up in Texas in the 1950s, I never thought of the preaching I heard every Sunday in my home church as "black preaching." I simply thought of it as preaching, and I thought it was the kind of preaching most people of faith heard on Sunday mornings. It was not until I began to venture out into the wider world that I discovered a distinct difference in the preaching of my pastor and the preaching of the pastors of my Mexican American and white friends. My church's worship services were lively, lengthy, emotional events, filled with joy and much celebration. From beginning to ending there was this constant verbal exchange between the pulpit and the pew. The "amen corner," consisting of the senior, most respected members of the church, was quite vocal in encouraging the pastor to "make it plain" when he announced the title of his sermon and began, as he would say, "to argue God's case." This weekly antiphonal exchange would ultimately end on a high celebratory note.

Each Sunday we waited eagerly for Pastor Henry Clay Dilworth Jr. to open the Scriptures and preach words of life to us. Seldom, if ever, did he disappoint. One Sunday we would be in the lion's den with Daniel and the next Sunday we would be shipwrecked on some distant sea with the apostle Paul, but on no Sunday were we left without hope. Each time Reverend Dilworth stood to preach, he provided an able and compelling witness to the power of God to watch over, deliver, and take care of God's own, just as he did in biblical times. He made the witness of Scripture come alive for us through his deep knowledge of the Bible, his wonderful ability to help us see ourselves in the Scriptures, his careful choice of words, his gestures and animated contortions, and his unending appeals for us to respond in appropriate ways to what God had done for us and also what God required of us.

I walked away from the worship service each week feeling that I had been in the presence of God in helpful and hopeful ways. In later years when I heard different types of preaching—some of which was quite understated—I came to appreciate more and more the amount of effort many black preachers put into their sermons. I also came to understand and appreciate the black context and the preacher's determination to address it head on. It is not a different gospel that blacks preach; it is simply the gospel filtered through their cultural context. It is this context-laden preaching that is typical of what one hears in black churches even to this day. Context drives the creative process. The essays in this book represent my ongoing effort to think through the contextual distinctions of African American preaching in an attempt to discover those multifaceted dynamics that constitute the essence of this style of proclamation. I continue to believe there is much in black preaching that is instructive for preaching in general.

Chapter 1 tells the story of my own preaching journey and how my life and ministry were shaped by the black community in the 1950s and 1960s. For many of us who came of age in those tumultuous decades, the church as institution was the only thing we had that we could truly call our own. Our lives revolved around it. We were shaped by it, and we bear the marks of its indelible imprint. Chapter 2 is a detailed account of the differences between black preaching and the homiletic theory taught primarily by white homileticians. Much of that theory, which is based on white religious experience, flies in the face of long-established preaching practices in the black church. Owing to this, black students who attend predominantly white seminaries and divinity schools are often left to piece together a workable homiletic that will fit the particulars of their own religious experience. Included in this chapter is an urgent plea for more dialogue between these two traditions that are so intricately linked to one another in American history and in current practice.

Chapter 3 provides a critique of the black worship experience and describes ways in which the black church can continue to be faithful to its calling to be the church of God in the twenty-first century.

Contrary to conventional wisdom, all is not well in the black church, which is not now, nor has it ever been, a monolithic institution. Many predominantly black American congregations are standing at the crossroads, attempting to chart a path between past experiences that helped to sustain the black church through some of the most tumultuous years in American history and an uncertain future in a rapidly changing postmodern world that celebrates difference, diversity, and otherness with little respect for or knowledge of the past. In this chapter I argue that as the black church seeks to remain relevant, it runs the risk of proclaiming another gospel that has at its center something other than the traditional Christian witness to Jesus Christ.

Chapter 4 addresses the future of preaching and the place of the black church in that future as Christianity moves closer and closer to becoming predominantly a religion of people of color in the global south. European missiologist Andrew Walls defines these people of color as the representative Christians of the twenty-first and twenty-second centuries. According to Walls, it is they who will set the theological agenda in the upcoming century. In this chapter I claim that North American blacks share some similarities with the people of color in the southern hemisphere and that we must continue to develop and strengthen those ties.

Chapter 5 describes the ways that the Scriptures function in black preaching and why the Bible continues to serve as the prism through which many blacks view their lives. Blacks, for the most part, do not make the mistake of worshiping the Bible, but they are more receptive to the preacher's invitation to enter into the world of Scripture and find, as Karl Barth says, "such answers to their questions as they deserve."[1] Owing to their desire to hear *from* God as opposed to merely hearing *about* God, the black construal of Scripture involves an interpretive strategy that renders the mighty sovereign present each time the word is proclaimed.

Chapter 6 describes how the black imagination works in the sermon-creation process and the different levels of imagination that many black preachers bring to a cyclical exegetical exercise and how the imagination is invited to the study table from the beginning to the end of the investigative process and even beyond. Chapter 7 focuses on the black preacher's love of crafted speech and the manner in which artful rhetoric testifies to the power of God. Even though much of America has moved beyond stylized speech, it continues to be a highly sought-after art in the black church. Preachers who are known for their ability to "say it," continue to hold many of the major pulpits in black America.

Chapter 8 describes my own method of sermon preparation and delivery. I place appropriate emphasis on exegesis and context, but I also take a careful look at the manner in which sermons are structured. I'm guided by what for me is a very simple truth: If you can see it, you can say it! Once the sermonic idea or controlling thought has been determined, I suggest a way of horizontally outlining the sermon that helps preachers to visualize its movement in a very clear and precise manner. Once the overall movement of the sermon has been laid out visually then scriptural exposition, illustrations, images, and picturesque speech can all be brought together in service to a sermon that flows in a logical but lively and creative manner.

Finally, in chapter 9 I list the ways in which both beginning preachers and preachers with years of experience can strengthen their preaching through ongoing critique and reflection. While the steps in this chapter may seem rather elementary to the more experienced preachers, this kind of careful review of the fundamentals of preaching can be quite instructive for young and old alike.

While some of the essays included in this volume have been published previously in other works, they are presented here with modifications and additional insights. The reflections in this book represent my effort to "testify" to the communicative power, imaginative insights, joyful celebration, and unabashed hopefulness that is heard in black churches throughout America. Testimony, according to Paul S. Wilson, is confession or witness that speaks of the faithfulness and steadfast nature of God. "The testimony may be the preacher's own or spoken on behalf of someone in the Bible or contemporary world."[2] The best of black preaching and the oratorical devices through which it is communicated are indeed testimony, for they witness to the power of God to provide, empower, and sustain a people historically and to this present day.

Acknowledgments

*T*his page constitutes a continuation of the copyright page. Grateful acknowledgment is made to the following for permission to quote from copyrighted material:

Excerpts from James Cleveland, "While I Have a Chance," © Martin & Morris Music Studio Inc. Used with permission.

Chapter 1, slightly revised here, previously appeared as Cleophus J. LaRue, "From Texas Pastor to Princeton Professor," in *From Midterms to Ministry: Practical Theologians on Pastoral Beginnings,* ed. Allan Hugh Cole Jr., © 2008. Wm. B. Eerdmans Publishing Company, Grand Rapids, Michigan. Reprinted by permission of the publisher, all rights reserved.

Chapter 2, slightly revised here, previously appeared as "Two Ships Passing in the Night," in *What's the Matter with Preaching Today?* ed. Mike Graves, © 2004 Westminster John Knox Press. Used with permission.

Chapter 3, slightly revised here, previously appeared as "Pulpits without Purpose," in *Our Sufficiency Is of God: Essays on Preaching in Honor of Gardner C. Taylor,* ed. Timothy George, James Earl Massey, and Robert Smith Jr., © 2010 Mercer University Press. Used with permission.

Chapter 5, slightly revised here, previously appeared as "African American Preaching and the Bible," in *True to Our Native Land: An African American New Testament Commentary,* ed. Brian K. Blount, Cain Hope Felder, Clarice J. Martin, and Emerson B. Powery, © 2007 Fortress Press. Used with permission.

Chapter 6, slightly revised here, previously appeared as "Imagination and the Exegetical Exercise," in *Best Advice: Wisdom on Ministry from Thirty Leading Pastors and Preachers,* ed.William J. Carl, © 2009 Westminster John Knox Press. Used with permission.

Chapter 1

One Preacher's Journey

I was born and raised in Corpus Christi, Texas, a seaport town near the southern tip of the state on the Gulf of Mexico. I came to faith in Calvary First Baptist Church under the same pastor who received my grandmother into the fellowship and baptized my mother and most of the LaRue/Rice offspring. I, along with other young people in my community, came up through what was then called "the total program of the church," which means we were involved in every aspect of the church's life—from Sunday school to Sunday morning worship, to the Baptist Training Union, and finally to the evening worship service. Just about every day of my life was spent being around, thinking about, or participating in something pertaining to church life. I understand that today my kind of church upbringing is rare, for many times we get people in seminary that were not associated with the church as children and only came to Christ through a Campus Crusade ministry or later in life as adults searching for more meaning in life.

Pastor Henry Clay Dilworth Jr. drilled the Scriptures into us at every opportunity. He told us to read the Bible before we read anything else in the morning. And that Bible we were instructed to read was none other than the King James Version. As a child, I just knew that was the version Jesus used. Along with the Scriptures, a healthy smattering of what Baptists believed and practiced was thrown in for good measure. Because the black church makes little distinction between the sacred and the secular, I learned to look for God's presence in every aspect of the human situation. Some mainliners are aghast when I tell them that politicians frequented our church and

1

were allowed to make their case on Sunday mornings. However, when they were done, Rev. Dilworth thundered a prophetic note of justice right in the faces of the squirming politicians. The National Association for the Advancement of Colored People (NAACP) was allowed to solicit memberships in the narthex on Sunday mornings, but they, too, were called to account by Rev. Dilworth if they did not speak up for the poor to his liking. From the participation of politicians, civic leaders, business people, and others in our congregation from time to time, I learned that nothing was off-limits for the church. The church's witness was meant to be heard and seen everywhere and in all places. I grew up believing that the church—the people of God—was to be involved in all of life as witness to God's rule and reign upon the earth.

My life and my ministry were shaped by the turbulent 1950s and 1960s. I was brought up in a low-income home with a mother, father, brother, and two sisters. The family, church, school, and community were the center of our daily existence. Although my parents struggled to make ends meet, life did not seem difficult to me as a child because everyone else in the community was pretty much in the same economic condition. As I look back on my childhood, I remember growing up in the segregated South as some of the happiest days of my life. I went to a completely segregated school for the first six years of my public education. I was taught by some of the most able black teachers of that day. They maintained class discipline with a stern look and a smooth paddle.

There was also a large Mexican American population in Corpus Christi, but the segregationists were so intent on keeping that system in place that we were not allowed to associate with the Mexican American children at school even though we all lived in the same neighborhood. The Mexican Americans had their school, and the blacks had theirs. They were within rock-throwing distance of one another, but contact was strictly forbidden, for Mexican Americans were recognized as white in the eyes of the law. The whites who lived on the other side of town were completely separated from us. Occasionally sporting events brought the races together, but such times were few and far between. We had no cafeteria at the all-black George Washington Carver Elementary School, so we had to use the cafeteria at the Mexican American school 150 yards away. Each day—in good weather or bad—our teachers lined us up and marched us across campus to the visiting cafeteria. But even then we were not allowed to eat with the Mexican Americans, for that, too, was against the law. The blacks had to wait outside until the Mexican American students had eaten and completely vacated the building before we were allowed to enter and eat our lunch. In later years both schools were demolished and replaced with a single structure. The new school took the name of the demolished Mexican American school while the name of the black school was dropped altogether.

I remember the civil rights movement and its impact on America, for it had an immediate effect on my life. With the passage of the Civil Rights Act in 1964 the public school systems of America started on their arduous desegregation tracks, even though they had been ordered by the Supreme Court to do so a decade earlier. Also, I vividly recall listening to Martin Luther King Jr. on television the day he gave his "I Have a Dream" speech from the steps of the Lincoln Memorial in August of 1963. I remember sitting in my fourth grade classroom the Friday we heard the news that John Kennedy had been shot. I also remember the Sunday in 1965 when Malcolm X was gunned down in Harlem and also how sick I felt the evening the news broke in 1968 that Martin Luther King Jr. had been assassinated. Bobby Kennedy's death a few months later rounded out that very troubled decade in American history. The Vietnam War was both real and frightening to me, for when I turned eighteen I took a bus downtown to register for the draft.

I have also felt the sting of racism and its dehumanizing effects. As an eleven-year-old boy, I remember traveling on a Greyhound bus to El Paso with my mother and other siblings to be reunited with my father, who had traveled there to take a better paying job at a steel mill. When it was time to reboard the bus on our layover in San Antonio, according to bus regulations, we were entitled to reboard the bus first since we were among the original travelers coming up from Corpus Christi. When the white driver saw a black woman and her four children trying to board the bus first, he became incensed, turned flush red, and ordered us to the back of the line. My mother— thinking he did not understand that we had ridden the early bus up from Corpus Christi—showed her ticket stubs and asked if she could reboard so we could be seated together. Visibly angry at this point, the driver shouted at my mother, "Hell no! I told you to get to the back of the line." He then took his forearm and forcefully shoved my mother aside. Without missing a beat, in a very different tone of voice, he turned to the white passengers and invited them to board the bus. My heart hurt for my mother. It was more than I could bear. I soon felt warm tears streaming down my face as we watched everyone else get on the bus, including the driver, who then ordered my mother and her four children to get on board or be left behind.

Needless to say, the rest of that much anticipated seven-hundred-mile trip was ruined. I couldn't help but wonder what we had done to make the bus driver so angry when we were simply following the rule of allowing originating passengers to reboard the bus first. I am not angry at the world for such incidents in my past, nor do I go around thinking about them every day. But I also cannot pretend that I have not been shaped by those incidents in ways possibly unknown to me. Without a doubt, they are a part of my context.

But raw encounters with racism have not been the whole story of my life. I love history today because a white seventh-grade teacher named Cappi Ascencio made the past come alive for me. Mrs. Ascencio, who loved to recount the battles of the Civil War, was in her element describing the strategies and eccentricities of the generals who fought those battles. I became interested in journalism because a white high school teacher named Bunny Steele had a knack for getting kids interested in the subject. I decided to attend Baylor University in Waco, Texas, because that's where Mrs. Steele had gone to school, and I majored in journalism because she made it so interesting and exciting to me. The worst scolding of my public school days came from Mrs. Steele when I intentionally missed my high school's award ceremony where I was to receive a top, statewide honor in journalism. I skipped the ceremony because I was afraid the other black students would laugh at me for being too bookish. Needless to say, Mrs. Steele was not happy. She saw right through my lame excuse and let me have it from all sides. While she talked to me, tears welled up in her eyes. I knew then she was upset with me because she cared about my future. In later years I would never make a major decision without picking up the phone to consult with her. Both women were quite helpful in my formative years. They were tough, insistent, and demanding on all of us, and they did not brook any foolishness when they thought you were not giving it your best.

I was admitted into Baylor because several white Southern Baptists took an interest in me. Glenn Huston, the local school board president, whose daughter had recently graduated from Baylor, was determined that I, too, would have the same chance as his daughter to get a decent start in life. Huston put me in touch with Ralph Storm, a Baptist layman and Baylor trustee who changed the trajectory of my life. Storm told me in later years that he "gently nudged" Baylor to reconsider my application after I was denied admission the first time I applied. His timely intervention taught me a very important lesson: To the extent that any of us succeed in life it is often because somebody helped us at a very critical juncture along the way. These stories and many more constitute my context. They have shaped who I am and how I view the world.

The Call to Christian Ministry

From my early teens onward I felt the call of God upon my life. But it was not until Rev. A. Louis Patterson, a gifted preacher from Houston, came to my hometown to preach the citywide revival that I accepted my call to ministry. Patterson made an indelible impression on me with his knowledge, commitment to excellence, and preaching gifts. He was a highly educated, extremely articulate person who preached the gospel with power and conviction. There were no histrionics and pyrotechnics in his preaching, yet his style was riveting and impressive. He stood and preached without notes in a reflective, thoughtful, and life-altering manner. Patterson became the connecting link between my past and my future in the church.

Often I had been disappointed with the backward-thinking, anti-intellectualism that was so typical of the black religious experience in Texas. Because of that kind of antiquated thought, I was convinced that God's call and claim on my life could not possibly involve ministry and most certainly not in Texas. In A. Louis Patterson, however, I found a model and mentor worthy of emulation. In time I would come under the influence of other significant preachers on the order of P. S. Wilkinson Sr., Manuel L. Scott Sr., Caesar A. W. Clark, James A. Forbes Jr., and Gardner C. Taylor. But as a nineteen-year-old young man still sorting through vocational choices, I saw in Patterson a healthy mixture of the old and the new; I saw in him what was best about the black church's past and most hopeful for its future. I announced my call to ministry one month after Patterson left town. I knew after listening to his preaching that my life would never be the same and was convinced that I would have to make the necessary sacrifices to prepare for ministry through formal study. Patterson made me know that school was not an option but a require-ment. The road to that education would be lengthy and circuitous, but it was one I knew I had to travel.

From Texas Pastor to Princeton Professor

In a manner of speaking, I put the cart before the horse as it relates to my seminary education and subsequent return to ministry. I moved in what many would claim to be the reverse order of the normal course of ministerial preparation since I was actively involved in pastoral ministry for fourteen years before I enrolled as a MDiv student at Princeton Theological Seminary. In my pursuit of a theological edu-cation, I moved from actual practice to theory and finally to reflec-tion on both practice and theory in my current capacity as a professor of homiletics.

An Early Spiritual Call and a Late Academic Start

I was called to the gospel ministry at the age of nineteen. Given the preeminence of preaching in Baptist circles, we usually referred to it as the call to preach. In black Baptist circles formal educa-tion was not a requirement for Christian ministry. That de facto rule had its strengths and weaknesses. As strength, it allowed a young, untrained minister to plunge immediately into the thick of minis-try. As a weakness, it left one without the benefit of a theological foundation in ministry and thus no means of engaging in informed reflection and formation on the how-to, why, and what of Christian ministry.

We literally learned to do ministry by watching and being watched by Rev. Dilworth. A number of us were in our teens when we announced our call, and one minister was as young as six when he was allowed to go forward in the expression and use of his preaching gifts. Our parents totally entrusted us to Pastor Dilworth's care and guidance. He was the worship leader each Sunday morning. He appointed the devotion leaders (those responsible for the preservice prayers and songs), and he decided who would participate in the worship service and where each participant's contribution best fit. He guided us not simply in the knowledge of the various functions of Christian ministry but in all of life. He instructed us on how to dress as well as how to conduct ourselves in the church and in the community. He insisted on a high standard of pulpit decorum and ministerial ethics. Rev. Dilworth was modest in his manner and frowned on any young minister whom he thought had gotten "a little too big for his britches." If he detected any sense of entitlement in his young understudies, he didn't hesitate to call us to account publicly and to insist that the offending minister mend his ways.

Rev. Dilworth was for many of us a walking seminary. He taught us the Scriptures on at least six different occasions through the week. He sat patiently with us and talked to us out of his vast wealth of experience about how to engage in effective pastoral care. He took us with him to visit the sick, the poor, and those who were struggling to overcome scandal or other unfortunate incidents in life. He was our first homiletics teacher because he critiqued all of our sermons and would not hesitate to stop us midway and ask us to sit down if he felt we had not made sufficient preparation. When it came time to license a minister, a positive church vote was never a foregone conclusion. Some ministerial candidates were sent back to ponder a while longer what they believed God had called them to do. To this day all the young ministers who went through that grueling process under Rev. Dilworth's guidance are still actively involved in ministry.

I pastored my first church just like Rev. Dilworth pastored my home church. He was the model of a successful minister to me in the early years of my ministry. However, I came in time to recognize that

I was doing ministry out of a preset mold, strictly by Rev. Dilworth's book. Even though his pastoral experience shaped a faith community for over fifty years, I came to realize that a mere imitation of his ministry would never allow me the freedom to be my own person. I would not be able to think through an issue on my own, for I had no training or skill in how to engage in informed biblical and theological reflection. I could only think by way of a template that had been established for me by a much-beloved pastor. To think within the confines of a box because one has no other choice is a restrictive process that causes ministers to become narrow in their clerical outlook. They are thus more likely to be threatened by change and the different perspectives that inevitably come before them in the very public sphere of Christian ministry.

Any matter that did not conform to my traditional understanding of the faith was suspect to me. I felt threatened because I simply did not understand how so-called Christians could see the world so differently from Pastor Dilworth and the tradition in which I was shaped. Consequently I felt I had no other recourse but to denigrate and speak disparagingly of anything different because I did not have the necessary tools to engage in theological vision and discernment. I didn't know how to think and reason theologically. I had no sense of the broader history of the church, no exposure to classical theology, and no skill in different approaches to Scripture, interpretive strategies, and other vitally important hermeneutical issues. And I was convinced that the kingdom of God consisted only of the National Baptist Convention and its few faithful adherents. To imitate a tradition in the name of faithfulness eventually smothers the one who has embraced it as a source of life and sustenance.

A Desperate Desire to Attend Seminary

In the two churches I pastored prior to coming to seminary, I experienced many things in pastoral ministry that I literally had no clue how to deal with and absolutely no theological skills for thinking through. I could only go on the previous pastoral experience of others or very painful trial and error, which more often than not hurt the people who were the object of the trial and victims of the error.

For example, in my early twenties I experienced one of the biggest church fights of my life, which could have been avoided with a better understanding of church polity and conflict management, and an understanding of systems and how they operate.

One time a little girl in our congregation was raped and brutally murdered. A neighbor who lived nearby was charged with the crime. The police waited for me to arrive before entering the house to tell the heartsick parents that their little girl had been found dead 150 yards from their home. I did not have the ability to deal with this horrendous tragedy in the lives of this distraught family or for the larger church family that agonized over this incident. I was literally flying by the seat of my pants. An informed understanding of issues surrounding grief and tragedy would have been most helpful to me in this situation.

For years young women in the congregation who became pregnant out of wedlock had to come before the church and beg the church's pardon. It was one of the most humiliating things I had ever witnessed in my life, even when growing up as a child in my home church. When I became a pastor, I continued to inflict this inhumane sentence on young women. No such out-of-wedlock apology was ever expected from the male offender. In my heart I knew this practice was wrong and wanted to stop it but did not have sufficient grounding in theology or pastoral care to do so. When we finally stopped, it came at a heavy price to the congregation, especially for those who felt the church's moral standards were being weakened. Again, I acted from gut instinct as opposed to informed theological insight.

My die-hard stance against women preachers was another area of my ministry that I so desperately wanted to change as a young pastor, but I simply did not know how to accomplish it without tearing my church apart. There were many in the congregation who were adamantly opposed to women taking any kind of leadership role that had traditionally been relegated to men. More often than not they based their discriminatory stance against women on the Scriptures. And to make bad matters worse, the Scriptures they cited were often interpreted by white fundamentalist preachers who were on the wrong side of all the social justice issues with respect to the advancement of black people in this country. Yet the black church used the biblical and theological arguments of conservative whites to bar black women from the ministry. I wanted to argue for women and against the tradition, but I felt I did not have sufficient biblical and theological grounding.

One night a quiet, unassuming member of our church was beaten to death by her husband. I had no sense of the telltale signs of her misery, but I learned later that other church members knew of the abuse. I always worried that there was nothing in my preaching or teaching to lead that woman to believe she could confide in me, and to this day I regret that I was not of more help to her in her struggle to break free from her repressive and abusive husband. Again, I knew I needed to broaden my preaching and teaching, but I simply did not know how.

In time I came to see that I was not really developing as a preacher. Even though my church provided me with a generous book allowance, I really had no idea of what kind of books to buy and why. I was not being educated in a particular school of theological thought but was instead being trained to imitate outstanding black pastors whom we knew and loved. I, along with many of my peers, had my own favorites in pastors, and I tried to imitate them in every way.

I also came in time to distrust my preaching in broader circles. I felt that I could handle myself in the small, regional south Texas circles in which I had grown up, but when opportunities came to preach before statewide audiences, I began to feel the weight of not having sufficient preparation. Moreover, preaching outside my African American context was an even greater challenge. It was pure agony trying to prepare for such occasions, and each time I had to do so, I was overcome by a deep sense of dread and despair. I decided from those gut-wrenching episodes that I could not be the most effective minister I could be if I did not take time out to prepare for Christian ministry instead of winging it by mimicking the preaching styles and experiences of others. I desperately wanted to attend seminary in order to determine if there was any method to this madness, in a manner of speaking.

I purposed in my heart to seek formal training no matter what the cost—even if it meant giving up my church and very fulfilling ministry.

A Second Chance to Prepare

When I finally began my studies in seminary in the 1980s, I had more hands-on pastoral experience than many of the professors who were teaching me. I had already pastored two Baptist churches in Texas— one with a membership of one thousand plus—and had participated at every level of my denomination's work and witness throughout the world. Entering seminary on the heels of two pastorates, I had already filed away over six hundred sermons, preached and/or participated in over four hundred funerals, and presided at an untold number of weddings and special-day celebrations. And all of this by the time I reached thirty. I came to seminary not out of a desire to learn how to do ministry but rather to be more effective in the ministry I was already doing. I in no way saw seminary as a repudiation of the ministry I had been involved in; instead I saw it in terms of strengthening and grounding the work I was already doing.

My student days at Princeton turned out to be a second chance at formal study. By the time I graduated from Baylor University with my undergraduate degree in the late 1970s, I was already pastoring my second church, Toliver Chapel Missionary Baptist Church. I felt, however, that my education would not be complete without a seminary degree. I wanted to commute ninety miles up the road to Ft. Worth, Texas, to attend Southwestern Baptist Theological Seminary. When I mentioned my plans to T. J. Montgomery Sr., my very supportive chairman of deacons, he informed me that he felt the church would not support such a move. Never really a fan of formal training, he said I already had more education than I needed to pastor people in central Texas. Thus, I gave up any hope of attending seminary and decided to pursue a graduate degree at Baylor instead. The church promised that if I stayed at Baylor, they would pick up all costs. I graduated a second time from Baylor in 1982 with a Master of Arts in religion. That degree was my consolation prize for not being able to attend Southwestern Baptist as I had originally hoped. The following year, still unable to move beyond the confines of Waco because of my pastoral responsibilities, I was accepted into Baylor's PhD program in church history. The workload of that program soon forced me to face up to the fact that I could not effectively juggle so many different responsibilities—family, church, school, community, and so forth. Though I had to drop out of the PhD program, I still could not bring myself to give up on the chance of a seminary education one day. Getting there, however, would not be easy.

John B. Davidson, a crusty but prescient religion professor at Baylor, watching me frantically jump from pillar to post, cornered me long enough one day to tell me what I already knew in my heart: I would have to content myself with being a pastor of a fairly sizeable congregation in central Texas or make a complete break with my church and head to a different part of the country where I could concentrate fully on my seminary education without the burden of pastoral responsibilities. By this time I had given up on attending a Baptist seminary in the mid-1980s because of the fundamentalist fight raging in Southern Baptist circles at the time. Professors for whom I had the highest regard, many of whom had given the best years of their lives preparing men and women for ministry, were hurt in that internecine conflict, and I wanted no part of it. Baylor Professors Daniel B. McGee and Ray Summers were among those encouraging me to move beyond the narrow confines of Baptist life. They urged me on as I pondered making that leap of faith from Waco to a different part of the country. Robert Sloan, a Southern Baptist graduate of Princeton Theological Seminary, had just been appointed to the Baylor faculty, and with his support I set my sights on Princeton, in large part because of its long-standing history of scholastic excellence and because I desired an academic environment where I could study and pursue learning without fear of reprisal.

Once ensconced in seminary, I always asked myself a couple of foundational questions in each and every class I was privileged to take: Will it fly in the black church? And is it something that would benefit, by which I meant uplift and transform, the people I have known and pastored in the years before I came to seminary? Those questions kept me centered and focused in my educational pursuits. They helped me not to forget the reason I always believed seminary was so important to my spiritual journey. I was there to learn how better to serve the church I knew and loved. I never lost sight of that. In that regard I was different from many of my classmates. I was reflecting on fourteen years of pastoral ministry while they, lacking the benefit of prior pastoral experience, were focusing on future possibilities for ministry.

No matter what you are exposed to in seminary, you must always keep before you the ultimate reason you are there. I wanted to learn how to be more effective in pastoral ministry and was never disappointed in that overall pursuit. For example, I could focus on people and actual situations as the professor talked about celebrating the Lord's Supper as a protest to the church's exclusivity and entrenched prejudices. While such lectures were provocative because of my previous experience as a pastor, I knew that the Lord's Supper was not the best place to protest wrongs in the black church. As professors talked about the different models of preaching, I knew there were people in my former congregations who were much more concerned about what I said as opposed to how I said it. I knew from experience if they heard a ring of truth in your preaching, you really didn't need an element of surprise to maintain their attention. They were simply glad to hear the good news. As professors introduced us to different ways of interpreting the biblical texts and as they pointed out things to me that I had never seen in the Scriptures, I was always thinking in the back of my mind, How would I preach this to my former congregations?

Much of what I learned in my classes was quite helpful. Suffice it to say, however, that some of what I was exposed to was so far off the mark that I would have been voted out of any black congregation the same day I tried to present it to them. I came in time to understand that one must make a distinction between what stretches you intellectually and what moves you beyond the bounds of the possible into the realm of the incredulous. I also came to understand that contextual decisions come into play when one is considering how to think through and apply the benefits of one's theological education. More importantly, there was never any doubt in my mind that I was preparing myself to be of service to the church. I suggest to all seminarians that they begin with the faith that was once delivered to the saints and work their way from there into new and uncharted waters.

I was exposed to much that broadened my understanding of the faith as well as the particulars of the practice of ministry. My exposure to Scripture and the biblical languages was both illuminating and empowering. To study the history of the church from its founding in the first century up to the present day gave me a sense of the breadth and depth of the church. Although I had been a pastor for fourteen years, the practical theology courses were enlightening and inspiring. The practice-preaching laboratory and the student-led critiques that came afterward strengthened me in my blind spots or in areas where I simply was not aware of a weakness. The theory behind the practice made sense to me. The professors I found most helpful were those who had some sense of the church: those who were intent on making a connection between what they were teaching and what we would be exposed to in the ministries for which we were making preparation. I was most fortunate to have this in Dennis Olson, one of my Old Testament professors. He never specifically said he was making a connection, but we all knew there was a point in his presentation when he stopped lecturing and starting connecting. We longed for those connections because in the early days we were not always able to make them with such precision and insight as the professor.

There were some things I desired in seminary that simply did not come to fruition. While biblical studies were quite helpful, I wished a few of the biblical studies professors could have taken my contextual point of departure more seriously. It seemed at times that a few of them went out of their way to belittle my faith tradition's understanding of the Scriptures as if no good had come out of my evangelical upbringing. I came to faith within the confines of a very conservative, black Baptist church. Although in time I wanted to break free and move beyond that tradition, I never wanted to abandon it completely. To have that tradition totally disregarded made me doubt what the clearly gifted professors were trying to impart to me.

A few took delight in stripping us of what they called our "Sunday school mentality." Yet they seemed not to understand that it was that mentality that brought many of us to the doorsteps of the seminary, seeking a more in-depth understanding of the faith that had been imparted to us by "the school master [the local church] that led us to Christ" (Gal. 3:24 KJV).

Also, there was little in seminary to help me specifically with a better understanding of my Baptist heritage. I knew that I was going to a seminary where the Presbyterian expression of the Reformed tradition was taught. But there was little there in the way of actual church practice with respect to the Baptist tradition that I found helpful. This was especially true with respect to the order of the worship service, ordinances of the church, Baptist polity, and other beliefs and practices. I found very little that would make me a better Baptist pastor and get me ready to take on a Baptist church immediately after leaving the seminary. As more and more students attend seminaries not of their own denomination, we run the risk of sending out ministers who have little or no knowledge of their own denomination and its requirements and thus little or no loyalty to its continuance. It may be that Baptists, Methodists, Disciples of Christ, and other denominations that have a large number of their students in seminaries of another theological tradition might need to require them to do a year of study at a seminary or divinity school of their own tradition.

As I wrestle with this question, I continue to be haunted by a young man who graduated from Princeton and received a call to pastor a Baptist church in the local area shortly thereafter. One afternoon he called me and asked me to help him with the basic requirements of pastoring. "What," he asked, "are those words that I'm supposed to say when I baptize a person on Sunday morning? And how do I set up and carry out the Lord's Supper on Sunday morning?" These questions came from one who had recently graduated from a seminary different from his own theological tradition. However, those Baptist people who called him to their Baptist church expected him to know the fundamentals of how to pastor their church—especially with respect to the worship experience on Sunday morning.

The particulars of one's denomination will become even more important in the coming years as fewer and fewer seminarians come to school out of religious backgrounds that provide a good foundation for the formation of their faith. The need to educate them in such matters becomes all the more important as it becomes apparent that they have not grown up in what we used to call "the total program of the church." How one overcomes this dilemma I am not sure. It should not be expected that Princeton Seminary would be charged with the responsibility of getting Methodists, Baptists, Pentecostals, Disciples of Christ, and a host of others ready to pastor churches within the particular dictates of those traditions. Yet not to have exposure at that preparatory stage to the particulars of those traditions means that people are being sent out to pastor with a very low level of proficiency in their denominations. And the people who call our students to pastor these churches are left to wonder what these Princeton-trained Baptists, Methodists, and Pentecostals learned while they were in seminary.

There was and remains a vast gulf between the letter and the spirit of my seminary education. Somehow or another I never felt the proper balance was struck. Having had experience in the work and witness of the church, I understood full well that seminary was not going to be a Sunday school class. I knew it would be a place to learn how to think critically, gather information, sharpen skills, and ground one's self in the basics of the faith, but I had not expected such a complete rejection of matters pertaining to the Spirit. More often than not I had the sense that it was only a matter of gaining information and that Spirit and mystery had little or no place in our pursuit of knowledge.

What Princeton Taught Me

I came to Princeton with a different set of concerns from the average seminary student. I did not come fretting over whether or not I had been called to ministry or trying to figure out what my gifts might be. Nor was I worried about whether I would be able to find a job once I had completed my studies. I received calls to seven different churches while I was studying at Princeton. In fact, I specifically remember that some of my grades suffered as a result of being on the road too often, preaching for and then trying to explain to inquiring churches why I could not accept their offer to become their pastor. After completing my formal studies, I decided to accept an invitation to join the faculty at Princeton Seminary. I see my role at Princeton as preparing women and men for leadership and service to the church.

Successful in my twenties by the standards of my denomination and considered an up-and-coming young minister clearly headed for bigger and better things (e.g., a larger church), I purposely chose to give it all up and head to seminary to be sufficiently grounded in the faith and to come to a deeper understanding of biblical studies, church history, theology, and, most assuredly, sound and informed reflection on the practice of ministry. To this day I do not regret stepping down from my pastoral charge in my early thirties and heading to seminary for what turned out to be an additional eight years of formal education. In some ways the experience was not all I thought it would be, while in others it was richer and more rewarding than I could have ever hoped. Though I entered Princeton as a second-career student, I came with a glad heart and an inquiring spirit, for I knew I had a lot to learn simply on the basis of what I had already been exposed to in the early years of my ministry.

Gardner C. Taylor, regarded by many as one of the greatest preachers in the twentieth century, invited me one day to preach at the historic Concord Baptist Church in Brooklyn, New York. On the way to the chapel for the afternoon service, Taylor turned to me and asked how many years I had pastored my church before heading to seminary. When I told him ten years, he shook his head in disapproval and said to me, "I don't think I would have stepped down after so many years." His comments crushed me because of the deep respect I had for this great preacher and because he had been so influential in my desire to further my theological education. Taylor thought about what he said for a moment and then turned to me once again and said, "I take that back. You have done a noble thing and God will not allow himself to remain in your debt. God will honor your sacrifice." Looking back now over nearly forty years of ministry, I, too, believe along with Taylor that preparation for ministry is a noble thing. And God will certainly honor the sacrifices we make in order to expose ourselves to that preparation.

Such is my journey to this point. It has taken me from Texas pastor to professor of homiletics at Princeton Theological Seminary. It has been a journey of great joy and great sorrow, of achievement checkered by failure and accomplishment marred by human foibles. Yet through it all there has been a measure of grace given to me. First Samuel 7:12 says: "Then Samuel took a stone and set it up between Mizpeh and Jeshanah, and named it Ebenezer, for he said, 'Thus far the LORD has helped us.'" Such is my testimony about my journey up to now: Thus far the LORD has helped me; thus far he has been faithful to his promises and steadfast in his love. Throughout this journey I have learned that when I'm able to look deeply within myself, I find much that is common to universal human experience, and it is from that well—common experience—that I draw many of the insights for preaching and the teaching of preaching that are found within these pages. They most certainly reflect my formal training in homiletics, but they also reflect the hard won experiences of my early years of pastoral ministry in Texas.

Chapter 2

Black Preaching and White Homiletics

*B*lack preaching sprinted across the threshold into the twenty-first century in far better shape than much preaching in predominantly white churches. Though far from perfect, it continues to be regarded in many circles as the most vibrant, imaginative, and communicatively effective preaching on the scene today. Over the past forty years, white homileticians have used such words as "crisis," "hemorrhaging," and "lifeless" to describe the preaching in their pulpits. Richard Eslinger was one among many who acknowledged that the preaching of the mainline churches was in crisis: "This awareness has been with us for a long time now, reducing pastoral morale and congregational fervor. But the way out toward new effectiveness in preaching is not yet clear."[1]

Even while taking note of the downward spiral in their own tradition, white homileticians saw in black preaching much that was admirable and attractive. David Buttrick in *Homiletic* said, "I have been influenced by the Black homiletic tradition. All things considered, it is probable that the finest preaching in America today is Black."[2] Leander Keck in *The Bible in the Pulpit,* in a comparison of black and white preaching, said, "One could show rather easily that preaching has lost its centrality in most mainline white Protestant churches, although it has never lost its place in black Protestantism."[3] Paul Scott Wilson characterized black preaching as arguably the strongest preaching tradition in the world while Richard Lischer said of the black church, "they remind us that the sermon is not a verbal essay but an oral performance of Scripture that includes the whole congregation"[4] Stephen Farris in *Preaching That Matters* made a case for analogical preaching, using as a prime example the sermon Martin Luther King Jr. preached in 1968 at the Mason Temple Church in Memphis, Tennessee, the night before he was assassinated. The Exodus analogy that King employed of leading the people to the mountain top, looking over, and seeing the promised land stood out for Farris as an example of what was best in the analogical preaching he was attempting to describe.[5]

Paige Patterson, of the predominantly white Southern Baptist Convention, in an apparent nod to hyperbole, said of black preaching, "When it comes to rhetoric, the best Anglo preachers on their best days don't preach as well as a good black preacher on his worst day."[6] It was the black preaching of the civil rights movement that caught the ear of David James Randolph as he sensed a new preaching coming to birth under the banner of the New Homiletic. In *The Renewal of Preaching,* first published in 1969, Randolph said,

> It is simply impossible to conceive of the present struggle for civil rights without the centrality of preachers and preaching in the movement. This central role is not one that came into being just recently. For long years preaching kept the soul of the [African American] alive, nourishing his spirit, enriching his vocabulary, and providing a means of expression and direction.[7]

When white homileticians engage in their critical reflection on homiletical theory and methodology, caveats and other exceptions must be inserted; for often it is the case that the reverse of what is being argued is true in black preaching. Again, Keck is helpful. Addressing the loss of confidence in mainline preaching, Keck notes,

> To begin with, many preachers today have lost confidence in the importance of preaching. . . . TV has made it ever more difficult for people to attend carefully to merely verbal communication, except perhaps for sports on radio. . . . This loss of attentiveness to verbal communication, to oral discourse, has eroded the place of the sermon. The black church is an exception, for there it is often customary for the congregation to participate in the preaching with "amens" and "right ons"; to some extent, the same must be conceded to white "Pentecostal" churches as well. It is the staid, sophisticated, main-line white Protestant churches that have been

most affected. The preacher knows this quite well, and sometimes painfully; it has eroded the sense that preaching is important.[8]

The accolades being heaped upon black preaching are not to suggest that this style of preaching is without its difficulties. An African American student minister said to a much-lauded black preacher in Brooklyn, "Pastor, I have never heard a bad black sermon." To which the venerable, old pastor replied, "Which rock have you been hiding under? I've heard lots of bad black sermons. I've preached quite a few of them myself." The seasoned pastor truly hit the nail on the head, for there is plenty in black preaching that is neither commendable nor worthy of emulation. One has only to tune in to Black Entertainment Television or a local cable TV channel to see questionable antics and unbridled heresy run amok in the black church.

All things considered, however, black preaching—if studied for more than its cosmetic effects of style and delivery or its most widely known feature of celebration—has something of note to contribute to traditional homiletics in the twenty-first century. While there is no shortage of laudatory remarks regarding black preaching, the problem is that there is little or no substantive engagement of black preaching on behalf of those who speak so movingly of its potency and persuasive power. The dangers inherent in such nonengagement are legion.

First, there is the danger that two very fine preaching traditions—so intertwined in the complex of American religious life, faith, and history—stand the chance of passing each other as two ships in the night. Historian Mechal Sobel notes the manner in which blacks have historically influenced white religious perceptions, values, and identity. According to Sobel, "Although two world views existed, there was a deep symbiotic relatedness that must be explored if we are to understand either or both of them."[9]

Second, there is the problem of "disconnect" in preaching classes. In seminaries and divinity schools throughout America, because of our inability to engage one another to the enrichment of all, what is being taught by white homileticians seldom rises to the level of black expectations. Blacks are often more advanced in their preaching skills and generally bring more practical experience to the preaching classes than their white counterparts. Blacks, however, like most students, are in need of a sounder footing with respect to biblical, theological, and hermeneutical matters relative to preaching. Hearing little about what they know (i.e., their black preaching tradition) causes them to turn a deaf ear to what they need (i.e., the informed insight of traditional homiletics).

While it is clear that blacks have benefited from the theoretical and methodological insights of the major homileticians of the past century, what is equally clear, at least from a black perspective, is that this learning has often been a one-way street. What was being taught in the classrooms always came *to* blacks *from* the majority culture as if white homileticians were the lone guardians of those standards by which we are to teach, gauge, and assess what constitutes good preaching. In preaching classes throughout America, twenty centuries of preaching could be taught without ever mentioning the name of a prominent black preacher. In some instances, white homileticians openly expressed their ignorance of black preaching and black preachers. And even more troubling, all too many indicated little desire to be exposed to what they clearly did not know.

In the waning years of the twentieth century, the name of Martin Luther King Jr. was invoked as an example of the finest in black preaching,[10] but, with rare exceptions, white homileticians seldom made any effort to look behind King in search of the tradition that shaped him and the long line of preachers he sought with such determination to emulate.[11] If, and when, they did get to blacks, the black preachers' limited contribution was "saved" for the end of the semester or the last day of the class as if preaching done by blacks was an afterthought or an also-ran to the major, white preaching story.[12]

Even now, as white homileticians search for new ways to reenergize their pulpits, a strong and vibrant preaching tradition—born in part in their own house—goes largely unrecognized in their midst. While it is not my desire to turn white preachers into black preachers or vice versa, I do believe both traditions can profit from each other's strengths and weaknesses as our multidimensional, diverse Christian church moves into its fifth century of preaching on American shores.

Where to Begin?

Some of the interchange can begin simply by asking why something that has clearly fallen on hard times in the white preaching tradition still works in black preaching. An example is Fred Craddock's dismissal of deductive preaching and the three-point sermon. Craddock rightly argues that not only the content but also the method of preaching is fundamentally a theological consideration. He notes that there are basically two directions in which thought moves: deductive and inductive: "Deductive movement is from the general truth to the particular application or experience while induction is the reverse. Homiletically, deduction means stating the thesis, breaking it down into points or sub-theses, explaining and illustrating these points, and applying them to the particular situations of the hearers."[13]

Craddock dismisses the three-point sermon as outdated, out of touch with the pew, and ill-suited to address modern-day listeners with its deductive approach, authoritarian stance, and deliberate naming of what the listener should take away from the sermon today. In the deductive sermon, he argues, there is no democracy, no dialogue, no listening by the speaker, and no contributing by the hearer. He claims that deductive preaching is flat, lacking in imagination, and creates passivity in the listeners. If the congregation is on the team, he writes, "it is as javelin catcher."[14] Craddock struck a nerve with white preachers, conservative and mainline alike, throughout America. He also had a great impact on the teaching of homiletics in seminaries and divinity schools in the last quarter of the twentieth century.[15]

So strong was Craddock's broadside against the deductive, three-point sermon and a poem that when I arrived as a student at Princeton Theological Seminary in the 1980s, the perception that the three-point sermon was long-since history hung heavily in the air. That perception struck me as quite strange because I'd just heard a three-point sermon the day before in one of New York City's premiere black churches. I immediately sensed a disconnect between what white homileticians were espousing and what was going on in the black church. Again, Craddock had valid reasons for moving away from that type of sermonic form in many white churches—the changing nature of language, the turn to the listener, a fear of concreteness, the inability to name God's presence in the lived experience of the human situation, and so forth.

In the black church, however, the deductive, three-point sermon simply did not have the same disastrous effects it apparently had in some white congregations. This idea of a boring preacher or an overly authoritarian preacher thundering broadsides to a disconnected, discontented audience is not what the three-point sermon wrought in the best of black preaching. Not then, not now. The three-point sermon in the black church is clothed in imagination, humor, playful engagement, running narrative, picturesque speech, and audible participation on the part of the congregation. Thus, it is not the three-point sermon that is out; instead, it is the *boring* three-point sermon that must go. Should blacks be exposed to other forms of preaching? Of course! But must we throw the three-point baby out with the bath in order to achieve this? I think not.

The differences between black and white churches regarding the three-point sermon and deductive preaching are striking and thus worthy of investigation. Why is it believed to fail in one church while it flies in the other? What can we teach one another about its use or lack thereof? In fairness to Craddock, to read him is to understand that he is speaking primarily to white preachers who are trying valiantly to lift their preaching out of the sermonic doldrums. However, when Craddock's method is taught in seminaries, those who teach it do not always specify that his concerns are addressed primarily to whites. That oversight is where the disconnect comes to the fore. Blacks who have had positive experiences with the deductive, three-point sermon feel unaddressed and left out of the homiletical loop. Or they are left with the uneasy feeling that the homiletics teacher is scratching where the black church is simply not itching.

Another example of differences between black and traditional homiletics is Buttrick's understanding of sermon introductions. In *Homiletic* Buttrick said of introductions,

> They give focus to sermons. . . . [They] should not give away the structure of the sermon ahead of time in a pedantic fashion. . . . A good rule for preachers as for poker players: Never tip your hand.

Introductions should not be too long inasmuch as getting into focus can be accomplished rather quickly. So, as a general guideline, introductions may run between seven and twelve sentences in length. The sentence count is not arbitrary. An introduction can scarcely function in less than seven sentences. At the same time, after more than a dozen sentences congregational impatience will usually set in.[16]

Such guidelines for novice preachers are sure to be helpful. But simply stated, one must include some additional criteria for introductions in black preaching. In black churches it is understood that the preacher is going to take his or her time in the introduction of the sermon. In a complete reversal of Buttrick's admonition, not infrequently some blacks actually state up front what they're going to talk about, and the people still listen.[17] Hard-and-fast rules about length, timing, and retaining elements of surprise are not strictly enforced in the black church. Why are black congregations willing to give their preachers more time? Are there different listening expectations? Is the congregation more willing to hear a lengthy introduction if they believe the preacher will make it worth their while before the sermon has ended?

I believe there are different levels of listening and expectation in black congregations. These levels are cyclical and not linear. This differentiation gives the preacher more time than would be allowed in the average white church. First, more time is allowed in setting up the sermon because the preaching event is a much-anticipated, central component in the black worship experience. If neo-orthodox theologian Karl Barth is right in his assertion about what the Reformers took from us—everything but the Bible—allowing ample time for the preaching of the Word is indeed a theological act.[18] Second, the cyclical levels of listening allow the preacher more than one chance to lose a congregation and pick them up again. Multiple chances to reignite a congregation's interest are apparently less tolerated in white churches.

Seldom is a sermon in the black church completely written off by the listeners at the outset—poor introduction notwithstanding. In fact, "Take your time, preacher" is the most common refrain heard in the congregation at the beginning of the sermon.[19] Levels of listening allow the parishioners to gain something from the sermon even when it violates every established rule of thumb relative to the introduction, body, and close. There is a sense in which the listener simply changes gears in order to accommodate the preacher's level of communication and clarity.

The first level is what I call *high alert*. This is the highest level of expectation. While it usually occurs at the beginning of a sermon, it may puzzle white homileticians to learn that sometimes it can actually take place near the end of a black sermon. High alert is that point in the sermon where listeners are willing to give the preacher a chance to address them in a meaningful, coherent, and challenging manner. They are listening attentively, attempting to figure out how the word of God has addressed them that day and what claim is being made on their lives. Some preachers can hold the congregation's attention from beginning to end while others need time to hit their stride. The listening gears in the black church give preachers and listeners time to adjust to one another's communicative style.

The second level is *pearls without a string*. When the black listeners make up in their minds that the preacher lacks coherence, logical flow, and initial purposeful encounter, they don't stop listening; they simply listen with different expectations. They change gears. The listeners decide to retrieve as much as possible from the sermon through the gathering of meaningful pearls here and there. Pearls are ideas and concepts that stand alone, unrelated, or at least unconnectable in the listener's mind to other parts of the sermon. But they are helpful nonetheless to the listener because they offer some word that is meaningful or enlightening, or that resonates with their lived experience. The listeners string together whatever words of truth, illustrations, or meaningful phrases they can in order to find something of worth in the sermon.

Third is *broken pieces*. This level represents a last-ditch effort on the part of the listener to salvage something of worth from the sermon. All hope is gone for some clearly defined, controlling thought. Even pearls without a string are in short supply. The listener is reduced to a search for that *one* thing that will bear the imprimatur of the sacred. It can be a line of truth, a slice of life, a well-timed cliché, or a sidebar illustration totally unrelated to anything concerning the title, focus, or announced intent of the sermon. Sometimes it is the preacher's manner of speech and affable personality that end up carrying the day—"Well, at least he was well-spoken and friendly"—which is to say, they found grace in his willingness to be present for God, though not necessarily in his preaching about God. Broken pieces point to a bit of something here and a part of something there. The listener is determined to ride some meaningful piece of truth to the shore of understanding.

Fourth is *clock watching*. At this stage of listening the clock is speaking louder than the preacher. The listeners have given up all hope that the preacher will have anything meaningful to say. They simply sit tight, content to run out the clock. If sympathetic, they give the preacher the benefit of the doubt, attributing the ineffectiveness to a busy week or a crowded schedule. If not, there is inward disgust and silent anguish at the poor performance of the preacher, who was given every chance from beginning to end to salvage the sermon. These are the four levels at work throughout the sermon. The employment of any level at any given moment helps the black parishioner retrieve something from even the most poorly constructed, poorly delivered sermon.

Is a sermon that requires the changing of so many gears the ideal sermon? Absolutely not! Do parishioners have a right to expect more? Certainly! And on most Sundays they get more. However, even on off Sundays the black church is determined to hear a word from God. Their desire to salvage something from every sermon is actually biblical in its roots and encouraging in its consistency:

> As the rain and the snow
>   come down from heaven,
> and do not return to it
>   without watering the earth
> and making it bud and flourish,
>   so that it yields seed for the sower and bread for the eater,
> so is my word that goes out from my mouth:
>   It will not return to me empty,
> but will accomplish what I desire
>   and achieve the purpose for which I sent it.
>
> (Isa. 55:10–11, NIV)

It is this text and its promise that keeps black congregants listening even when they have every right to tune the preacher out. To dismiss the preacher out of hand at the introduction simply doesn't allow enough time for these traditional levels of listening to kick in. To institute hard-and-fast rules is to suggest that the black parishioner has only one level of listening—*high alert!* It also suggests low levels of expectation.

These are just two examples of ways the two traditions could be helpful to one another. Eugene Lowry's reversal and element of surprise,[20] Paul Scott Wilson's four pages of the sermon,[21] Thomas Long's brainstorming and claim of the text,[22] Charles Campbell's understanding of what it means to "preach Jesus,"[23] and the traditional understanding of what constitutes the gospel and/or proclamation[24] are all open for discussion and could profit from a healthy engagement with the black preaching tradition. And vice versa. All of these scholars have made valuable contributions to contemporary homiletics. To highlight bits and pieces of their works may seem unfair. That is not my aim. These critiques are not intended to be exhaustive; rather, it is hoped that they will foster more discussion between the traditions, not less.

How Blacks Learn to Preach

Another striking difference between black preaching and white homiletics is the manner in which blacks learn to preach. Separate and apart from matters of form, structure, content, and style, the entire black approach to the teaching of preaching differs markedly from the established pedagogy in traditional homiletics. Why is it the case that many blacks continue to learn to preach primarily through *emulation* of accomplished preachers they have come to admire? To emulate is not to copy but rather to set a standard of achievement by which one gauges one's own preaching ability and advancement. Does learning by listening suggest that blacks are anti-intellectual and thus unmindful of the importance of gaining a seminary-trained foundation in preaching?

The black church believes that teaching people to preach is fundamentally an ecclesial act and thus by its very nature a pedagogical function that the church cannot relegate to the academy alone. If indeed the Scriptures belong to the church, then the church cannot abdicate its responsibility in the guidance of those who will explicate those Scriptures in the name of the church. That blacks continue to learn to preach by listening to those whom they admire and respect—who are for the most part accomplished preachers who have received the approbation of the churchgoing public—is a theological act of the highest order.

That the black church continues to call and promote those who have been trained to preach in this manner is, I believe, its way of saying that it will have a determining voice and a controlling hand in the formation of those who advance through its ranks. This is especially true in the present era when modern biblical scholarship has sought in many ways to relegate the church's understanding of Scripture to "interpretive irrelevance."[25] For the most part, whites in mainline and high-church congregations are declared fit to preach once they have successfully completed the degree requirements of a bona fide theological institution and passed the basic exams required by their particular judicatories. Many are not even eligible to be considered for the top positions in churches until this part of their education has been successfully completed. Thus, they come to their charges, for the most part, with very little preaching experience.

In this respect blacks have the advantage over their white counterparts, for they have been trying their hand at preaching under the watchful eye of a local fellowship or judicatory since the announcement of their call. The black church, while not nearly as adamant about formal training as they should be, does not view such training as a replacement for its role in the formation of the preacher. It continues to administer its very vital function of shaping, directing, and teaching the newly called preacher of the gospel.

In many black churches, and in some white churches as well (white Baptist, Methodist, and Pentecostal, to name a few) the preacher is encouraged to go to school, but the lack of formal training does not prevent one from taking on preaching assignments and responsibilities. While the black preacher is clearly better off with the formal tools of investigation and the in-depth theological insight one receives through the successful completion of a certified theological program, the black church sees its role in the training of the minister as equally important.

Might not there be room in the academy for the surefire experience of seasoned mentors alongside the formal training that is currently taught? Young preachers need exposure to experienced pastors who can pass on to them not merely a skill but a way of life, a preaching *habitus*, if you will. We can no longer assume that those who sit before us in preaching class come to us with a good foundation in the life, witness, and ministerial practices of the church. It is here that the seasoned pastor, on the craft in the stream, can be of great help to those who are just beginning to try their hands and their hearts at preaching.

In many white churches one is declared fit to preach through *certification*. In the black church one is declared fit to preach through *demonstration*. In the former you have to show that you have been appropriately exposed to the fundamentals of preaching, while in the latter you have to show that you actually have some proficiency in the preaching act itself.

Blacks are coming more and more to appreciate and require that their preachers be formally trained in accredited theological institutions. And rightly so! The church benefits greatly from the minister who has experienced the formal study of a theological seminary or divinity school. The preacher's overall ministry is strengthened when he or she has been exposed, in a formal way, to biblical studies, church history, theology, and practical theology. Such study makes for a more grounded preacher, and it creates in the person of the preacher an enhanced capacity for theological vision and discernment. That said, however, a degree alone will seldom get the minister a job in a black church. Ministers have to demonstrate, or at least show promise, to pulpit committees and congregations alike that they can carry the weight of the pulpit. Most black churches continue to put preaching skills high on their must-have list when searching for a pastor.

In summary, preaching and the training of preachers is an ecclesial function that the black church is hesitant to surrender wholly to the academy. The black church takes its role in the education of the preacher seriously. I believe this is one of the reasons that there continues to be a strong preaching tradition within its ranks. Could not we all benefit if we thought more deeply about how to maintain these two very important pedagogical functions—the formal teaching of homiletics in the seminary coupled with some exposure to the impressionable powers of observation, participation, and subsequent mastery that reside in the accomplished preacher/pastors of our day?

What Is Black Preaching?

Granted, even while attempting to make a case for a more serious engagement with the particulars of black preaching, I must acknowledge that blacks themselves are not in agreement about how we define *black preaching*. (Neither is traditional homiletics of one mind about its preaching.) Nor are blacks in agreement on a unified definition of *the black church*. Many among us say there's no such entity. With the inclusion of white religious bodies with significant African American memberships, blacks belong to over two hundred denominations in the United States alone.[26] And as of 1997, church-going blacks in America claimed to have over 25 million members in more than 63,000 congregations.[27] While most blacks belong to predominantly black denominations, a sizeable number are in predominantly white denominations and would take exception to being left out of the definition of what constitutes membership in *the* traditional black church.

C. Eric Lincoln and Lawrence Mamiya, in their seminal study on the black church, maintained that in general, any black Christian person is included in the black church if he or she is a member of a black congregation, denomination not withstanding. However, in their book *The Black Church in the African-American Experience* they chose to limit their operational definition of "the black church" to the seven independent, historic, and totally black-controlled denominations: three Methodist conferences, three Baptist conventions, and the Churches of God in Christ.[28] Many would say their operational definition of the black church is too narrow.

With respect to the question of what constitutes "black preaching" there is a very powerful and settled school of thought amongst black preachers that says there is no such thing as black preaching per se, with its own specific characteristics and distinctive traits. Those who maintain this view say there are black preachers who preach, but they don't preach black; they simply preach the gospel. Chief among the proponents of this position was the late Samuel DeWitt Proctor, pastor emeritus of the Abyssinian Baptist Church in New York and professor of the Martin Luther King Chair in Ethics at Rutgers University.

Proctor, though not against black preaching, simply believed there was too much diversity within the tradition historically or as presently constructed to make accurate generalizations. Proctor observed that African American preaching demonstrated the same diversity as other forms of American Christianity and should not be characterized by style of delivery or theological assumptions.[29] His books on preaching were simply titled: *Preaching about Crises in the Community* and *The Certain Sound of the Trumpet.* His autobiography was titled *The Substance of Things Hoped For.*[30] Although he cowrote a volume of sermons with William Watley titled *Sermons from a Black Pulpit*, he was uneasy with the characterization of black preaching as a distinct body of literature to be studied and reflected upon.[31]

Others in black religious circles, while not as outspoken as Proctor, were also hesitant to style their works on preaching as peculiarly or uniquely black. Gardner Taylor, regarded by many as the dean of black preachers, titled his Lyman Beecher lectures in book form simply *How Shall They Preach.*[32] Taylor quotes more European preachers than he does black preachers or black homileticians in his book. Another black preacher/homiletician who comes to mind is James Forbes. Forbes titled his work on preaching *The Holy Spirit and Preaching.*[33] He has been described as the first contemporary "crossover" preacher in his ministry to the multiracial, multidenominational Riverside Church in New York City. The term *crossover* means that he was intentionally seeking to have broad appeal to as wide and diverse an audience as possible.

Even the black neo-Pentecostals and evangelicals on the order of T. D. Jakes and Bishop Paul Morton have made an effort to steer clear of racial designations in many of their published works. Some out-and-out deny any such characteristics exist while others simply move away from explicit references in an effort to broaden their appeal.

There are those, however, who believe there are sufficient characteristics in this style of proclamation to warrant the title "black preaching." This is not to suggest that the things that go on in this style are unique to black preaching or done by all black preachers, but it is to say that when taken together they come to the fore with such clarity and presence that one would not err in saying that these are some of the things you find repeatedly in the best of black preaching.

Characteristics of Black Preaching

The multiple characteristics of black preaching are cited here more as a starting place for those interested in learning more about the black preaching tradition than as a stopping point for what blacks have to contribute to the homiletical discussion. William B. McClain in the *Renewal of Sunday Worship* lists the following as characteristics of black preaching: biblical emphasis, prophetic preaching, poetic style, dialogue, preaching that is declarative rather than suggestive, and preaching that is life situational and contains some element of hope.[34]

James Earl Massey, in *The Responsible Pulpit*, lists five insights from the black preaching tradition with respect to the sermon: 1) The sermon is *functional* in that it is always regarded as a means to an end. 2) It is *festive* in that it deals with concrete life and aims to be an invitation to joy even in the midst of sorrow and struggle. 3) It is *communal* in that it must aid the sense of group life. 4) It is *radical* in that it seeks to confront the hearers in the very depths of their beings with the issues of life. 5) And finally, said Massey, the black sermon is *climactic* in that it seeks some type of celebratory close to make an impression on the hearers.[35]

Henry Mitchell, the foremost proponent of black preaching over the past three decades, made "celebration" the cornerstone of his homiletic.[36] In a later essay in the *Concise Encyclopedia of Preaching,* Mitchell listed three chief characteristics of preaching in traditional African American churches. First among the characteristics was intonation or "whooping"—the chanting or sing-song style of delivery in black preaching. Second was spontaneity, by which he means the ability to respond to the movement of the Spirit among preacher and congregation and to express deep feeling without shame. Third was the basic structure of the sermon, which Mitchell characterized as imaginative, narrative, and prone to generate an experiential encounter.[37]

Evans Crawford and Thomas Troeger in *The Hum: Call and Response in African American Preaching* cite participatory proclamation, or what some refer to as call-and-response, as a distinctive feature of African American preaching.[38] In Crawford and Troeger's work, those unfamiliar with the tradition are able to gain some insight into the antiphonal nature of the black worship experience as well as see how preacher and people give life and encouragement to one another at the preaching hour. They draw on five distinct phrases to demonstrate how participatory proclamation is brought to life in the black church: "Help him Lord!"—"Well!"—"That's alright!"— "Amen!"—"Glory Hallelujah!"[39]

Others have characterized a high regard for Scripture, a creative use of language, an appeal to emotions, and the granting of a certain authority or freedom to black preachers as significant characteristics. In an earlier work I, too, made an attempt to list the characteristics I considered to be foundational to this style of preaching. I argued that distinctiveness was not simply in the black style of delivery or manner of preaching but, more importantly, in our content.

When blacks respond enthusiastically in their worship settings to the preached word, they are not merely caught up in the emotions of the moment. They are, in part, responding to content shaped by a very powerful oral delivery. Among the distinctions in matters of content, I cited a biblical hermeneutic of a sovereign God who acts powerfully on the part of the disinherited and five realms or domains of experience into which and out of which blacks are shaped by the gospel and their lived situations.[40]

All such characteristics can only be described as touching different parts of the elephant.[41] They are, however, important places to begin the interactive quest. Moreover, substantive books on black preaching and books on preaching written by blacks abound, and they simply await engagement by the traditional homileticians. To the benefit of all, some have already begun this process of intersecting and interacting with black preaching. The act of preaching and the teaching of preaching can only be the better for it.[42]

To Begin Again

American Protestant preaching will surely be strengthened by the enhanced reflection and the continuous interaction of these two very fine preaching traditions. In the twenty-first century it can no longer be a one-way preaching street, with white homileticians on the sending end and black preachers on the receiving end. In the immediate future, seminaries and divinity schools will need to rethink staffing needs not just so that blacks can have someone in preaching who understands their tradition but also so that whites and others might be exposed in a formal way to the best insights of a vibrant preaching tradition of long-standing in their own midst. Those who resist and refuse the imminent changes upon us could find themselves speaking into a smaller and smaller circle.

The parameters of homiletics are ever expanding, and contextuality will be the name of the game in the years to come. Hispanics, Asian Americans, Native Americans, and others will have much to contribute to this discussion. A healthy appreciation of and lively exchange between all homiletic traditions will make for stronger preachers irrespective of ethnicity, gender, regional differences, and denominational ties. The teaching of preaching in the future, if it is to be effective, will have to reflect the broad and rich diversity of the global village that is now so clearly upon us and so much a part of who we are. Celebrating and building on our diversity are among the things most needful in our preaching today. If, indeed, all roads lead to preaching, then homileticians should take the lead in showing the church a more excellent way.

Chapter 3

Pulpits without Purpose

One

One morning, in a small village at the southernmost tip of India, I sat across the breakfast table from an Indian scholar who had just completed a book on preaching in the Indian context. On learning that I taught preaching in an American seminary, he leaned across the table and told me that during his research on preaching throughout the world, he had come to the conclusion that white American mainline preaching was in trouble because it focused too much on process and not enough on purpose.[1] He said he thought that American homileticians tended to focus too much on the how-tos of preaching and not enough on the whys and wherefores. Moreover, he thought Americans were bogged down in form and structure but seriously lacking in biblical depth and substance. While he was much more positive about the preaching of black Americans—especially the preaching of the civil rights era—he thought blacks, owing to their proximity to white mainline preaching, were also in danger of adopting the practice of preaching from what he called "pulpits without purpose." Pulpits without purpose happen when preachers neglect their primary mission—to preach the unsearchable riches of Jesus Christ.

While I cannot speak for Indian preaching or to the decline of white American mainline preaching, I do believe that if African Americans are not careful, we will indeed be guilty of mounting pulpits without purpose. I believe that the world is changing about us so quickly, that we are so caught up in the new and the now, and that we are so faddish to a fault, that it is all too easy to forget our primary reason for standing behind that sacred desk every Sunday morning. I understand that everything changes and nothing stays the same. I understand that there is no single way to preach Jesus. And I know there is nothing wrong with new ways of preaching Jesus, as long as it is Jesus who is being preached.

Anyone who is at all attentive to the present church scene must be aware that in every denominational tradition new forms of congregational life and new challenges to many long-established church practices are emerging. The signs of change are visible in all areas of church life. Our traditional churches now stand alongside seeker churches, cell churches, mall churches, seven-day-a-week churches, next churches, nondenominational churches, and even parachurches. Whatever we choose to call these new and different—and, in some cases, large and fast-growing—nontraditional congregations, they probably are the most visible and talked-about new church forms of the past thirty years.[2] Some say the fact that they are relatively new allows them to be more creative, more cutting edge, and more open to change than traditional churches. Many a young pastor has run into difficulty trying to move a traditional church along too hurriedly. Some pastors resign in disgust, and some are voted out in disgust. Others stand and fight and take the spoils of victory or the remnants of defeat. Still others simply step down and organize a new work in what they call "a different part of Zion." Suffice it to say, our churches are changing.

Not only are there changes in our churches, but there are also changes in our worship practices, including liturgy, music, and preaching. Although some congregations seek to retain their long-standing traditional liturgical practices, most are in great flux. Many congregations, especially those influenced by the "seeker church" movement, have thrown out their traditional liturgical practices in an effort to reach the baby boomers and Generation Xers who have left the church in significant numbers in recent years.[3] Still other congregations have kept traditional services intact but have introduced alternative worship as a way to satisfy different constituencies within the congregation. Many are characterizing these services as either *traditional* or *contemporary*.

All around us, churches are experimenting with worship, trying to discover what works and what does not, what will draw people and what will drive people, what will make them come in the first place and come back in the second place. Such experiments with worship frequently lead to conflicts, which some have referred to as "worship wars." In other churches there also have been disputes about traditional language about God. Some say they are uncomfortable with the traditional Trinitarian language of God the Father, the Son, and the Holy Ghost, preferring instead Creator, Redeemer, and Sustainer. Some even go a bit further, preferring Mother, Lover, and Friend.

Some churches have rewritten many of their old hymns, and some have discontinued certain well-loved hymns that they say are offensive to some because of their language and imagery. Some have rewritten "Amazing Grace" because it has the word "wretch" in it; they claim some people in this day and time may take offense at being referred to as a "wretch."[4] Some churches have discontinued singing "Onward Christian soldiers, marching as to war" because they say it encourages military aggression.[5] On the other hand, some hold fast to the old hymns, refusing to change one iota. A Presbyterian pastor in Philadelphia who refused even to consider a genre of music other than the old traditional hymns said he simply could not bring himself to sing what he called "that 7-11 music—the same seven words eleven times."[6]

Pentecostal practices are having a significant impact on African American congregations in storefront and traditional churches across the denominational spectrum. As Jackson W. Carroll points out, this neo-pentecostal movement—especially as manifested in some of the African Methodist Episcopal churches—combines a deep pentecostal piety with involvement in progressive politics and political activism, including a particularly strong concern for the plight of African American men.[7]

In recent years there has been an explosion of African American worship on television.[8] Although being on television, in and of itself, is not a bad thing, the desire to copy what is seen on television, without any kind of theological filter to separate the wheat from the chaff, can have a debilitating effect on unsuspecting congregations. Television is, by its very nature, an entertainment medium, and owing to its widespread influence in our lives, we are in danger of amusing ourselves to death.[9]

One night as I watched a sermon on television, I noticed people walking up to the pulpit area and throwing money at the preacher's feet while he was preaching. I wondered about the theological significance behind that act. Just because you see something on television is no guarantee that there is a theological justification for the act itself. Without a doubt, television is here to stay, but we must think theologically, critically, and reflectively about its use in our religious experience. It is a medium that has transformed our culture and set us on an uncertain course, and if we are not careful, "TV religion" could become just one of any number of ways that we seek to entertain ourselves.[10]

Two

All of our worship practices are caught up in change. Many church leaders desire to stay relevant by keeping up with the times and trying to stay at the forefront of new ways of worship, while other churches resist change completely. But change is nothing new in black churches. It has been with us in every age, although it has always been difficult to implement change in established, traditional, institutional churches. For example, historians point out that in the nineteenth century some in the African Methodist Episcopal Church did not approve of organs and choirs, considering them to be the work of the devil. Some clergymen, such as Bishop Henry McNeal Turner, thought the clergy should wear robes to give greater dignity to the worship service. But although AME bishop Daniel Alexander Payne believed that the AME Church should have educated ministers and dignified services, he opposed robes for AME clergy, preferring instead the plain dress of Richard Allen.[11] Moreover, Bishop Payne favored a strict adherence to the worship service outlined in the AME discipline and was, therefore, opposed to dance, song, and spirit possession.

Payne especially disliked the ring shout practiced by some black Methodists, where the participants clapped their hands and stamped their feet until they were overcome by the Holy Spirit, and he also opposed the singing of cornfield ditties such as "Ashes to ashes, dust to dust, if God won't have us, the devil must."[12] Payne thought such rites were "ridiculous and heathenish"[13] and did more harm than good, for in his eyes such carrying on disgraced and corrupted black Christianity. Another controversy was raised during the period after the Civil War, when some northern AMEs wanted to drop the word "African" from the AME name.[14] The point I'm trying to make is this: There have always been disagreements about the best way to be the church and to have church in the black church.

The black Baptists have also had their difficulties with change.[15] Gospel music and gospel choirs, for example, cramped the style of many black Baptist churches in the first half of the twentieth century. So offensive was gospel music to some in mainline American black Protestantism that some churches were known to throw out the gospel singers. Michael Harris, in *The Rise of Gospel Blues,* reports that one of the gospel singers who got thrown out of church in the early part of the twentieth century was a woman named Mahalia Jackson. Shortly after moving to Chicago from New Orleans, Jackson joined a group named the Johnson Singers, which sang gospel music throughout the city. But when a Chicago pastor heard this new type of music called *gospel* music, he was so offended that he threw Jackson and her group out of his sanctuary, saying, "Get that twisting and jazz out of this church."[16] On her way out the door, Jackson looked back at the pastor, no doubt in a tone of defiance, and said, "This is the way we sing down south."[17] But still, she was forced to leave the church.

In every age, as new ways of having and being church emerge, there will always be some resistance. In our rich black religious history, a group of congregants who decided to wear pulpit gowns on Sunday met with some resistance. And when another group decided to put a pipe organ in the church, they met with resistance, too. There will always be people who try to hang on to the old and others trying to break forth into the new, and both groups mean well. All sides must remember that many find it difficult to keep up with or to become comfortable with rapid and relentless change. Traditional church is an institution, and the nature of institutions is that they move slowly. What are we to make of all the changes that are upon us now, and how are we to deal with them? First, we need to understand that change will always incite resistance from some congregation members. Anything new or different will rub some people the wrong way, and they will try to resist the change, usually by saying, "But we have never done it that way before around here." Or they will say, "This is a Bible-believing church, and we have a certain way of doing things around here," suggesting that their church traditions strictly follow the Scriptures. But neo-orthodox theologian Karl Barth has reminded us that "there has never been . . . an intrinsically sacred sociology of the church."[18] No full-blown, biblically mandated way of having church is outlined in the Scriptures.

Congregational patterns and practices in Christian churches have not only varied considerably over time, but they have also differed substantially within each given time period. Church practices run the gamut, and they are less and less dictated by denominational beliefs and more and more influenced by the customs we see in churches in our local area or models we pick up at conferences or on television.[19] Sometimes we initiate a change in our churches simply because we don't want the pastor down the street to get too big a jump on us in implementing something new that might prove to be effective. But although change will frequently trigger some kind of resistance, we must remember that just because a tradition is long-standing does not make it biblical, and just because something is new does not make it unbiblical.

Second, we must also understand that even though some in our congregations will always resist change, some changes are unavoidable in our current, rapidly changing era. We are living in a posttraditional age. The term "posttraditional" does not suggest that we have moved beyond tradition but that we have moved to a place where inherited traditions are likely to play increasingly less decisive roles in the way we understand and order our lives. Time-honored ways of doing things change, and we have to adjust to that.[20] There was a time when women did not wear slacks to Sunday worship and both men and women might be asked to leave the church for attending "the moving picture show." There was a time when black Baptists did not applaud in church; instead, they said "Amen" because applause was considered appropriate for an audience being entertained, not for a congregation engaged in the worship of God. There was a time when some churches held fast to the closed Communion rule, and if you were not a Baptist in good and regular standing in that congregation, you could not participate in the Lord's Supper. There was a time when some churches would serve the Lord's Supper only on Sunday evening, because they said "supper" was an evening meal and was not supposed to be eaten at midday. But things change, and we must learn to separate custom and tradition from the nonnegotiables of the faith.

Many people now feel that a variety of traditions no longer carry the weight they once did. People are guided and directed more by an inward authority. No longer do we rely without question on traditional formulae for doing things or on long-established institutions and their representatives to give us directives for living or for how to have and be the church. Today, people rely on themselves and their own experiences to find appropriate ways to respond to the changes and challenges that arise in their lives and in their church experiences, and this approach is likely to continue in the future. Change is upon us, and we can no longer exert the kinds of controls over our congregants that we used in the past, when we could simply tell them, "The church says."

Third, as we try to deal with the changes and challenges that are upon us, we must never forget whose church it is in the first place. If we forget to whom the church ultimately belongs, we run the risk of preaching from pulpits without purpose. Jesus said, " 'Upon this rock I will build my church and the gates of hell shall not prevail against it' " (Matt. 16:18, KJV). Before we get all hung up about who's up and who's down, who's packing them in and who's barely hanging on, who has correctly perceived which way the winds of change are blowing and who is being left on the steps of yesterday's Holy Ghost headquarters—before we get caught up in all of that, we need to remember whose church it is and to remind ourselves that it really does not belong to us. I know some people who have been at their posts for so long that they begin to refer to it as "my church." But it really does not belong to us. Throughout Christian history there has been a rhythm to church life and church growth. Church existence and continuation are not solely in our hands; churches come and go, they start up and die out, they rise and fall, sometimes because of what we do and sometimes in spite of what we do.

Three

The missionaries from centuries past who sailed the seas and traveled through terra incognita (unrecognizable territory) to carry the good news of Jesus Christ did not have near the anxiety we have about what it takes to evangelize the world and to nurture, grow, and develop a church in the midst of changes and challenges. They knew better than so many of us today that they did not have the final say over the church's ongoing vitality and strength, because they knew it did not belong to them. As European missiologist Andrew Walls points out, those missionaries, when seeking to determine the efficacy and effectiveness of their work in Christ, were guided by three tests. I commend those tests to you today.[21] The first was the *church test.* The first sign of the legitimate expansion of the influence of Christ is the presence of a community of people who willingly bear his name.

The second test the old missionaries used to determine the efficacy and effectiveness of their work in Christ was *the kingdom test.*[22] The kingdom test stands for signs of the kingdom of God within your midst. Some church folks do not like signs of the kingdom because they are more interested in attending glorified social clubs than they are in attending to the inbreaking activity of God. But kingdom movements call the church to repentance and to alertness to the presence of Christ within.

Finally, there is a third test the old missionaries used—the *gospel test.*[23] The gospel test asks, Is Jesus Christ being preached within our midst? You cannot build a church on announcements and extracurricular activities. No church can be stronger than the gospel it proclaims. The church lives in her preaching—always has and always will.[24] Luke said Jesus came preaching and teaching. Paul said it pleased God through the foolishness of preaching to save those that believe. P. T. Forsyth said that with its preaching, Christianity stands or falls.[25] Paul Scherer said Jesus always knew what came first, so with confidence he turned to those around him and said, " 'As ye go . . . preach.' " (Matt. 10:7).[26]

In our ever-changing world, if we forget to preach Jesus and his crucifixion, we run the risk of preaching from pulpits without purpose even though our churches may be on the cutting edge of change and bubbling over with worldly success. To preach Jesus in this post-Christian world is our most compelling challenge and charge, for there is still power in the heart of that old story: For us—he took a birthday in time and was born of suspect parentage, in a third-rate country, in a forgotten corner of the world. He gave up his rightful seat in that celestial city that was older than Eden and taller than Rome. He traded in the praises of angels for the sin-stricken curses of lost humanity. He traded in a crown for a cross and a throne for a tomb. For us—Jesus the judge was judged in our place. And for us—God raised him from the dead on the third day morning. Amen![27]

Chapter 4

The Shape of Colored Preaching
in the Twenty-first Century

Colored preaching, by which I mean preaching done by people of color, is the preaching of the future. Colored preaching is the preaching that will be heard by a majority of the Christian world in the twenty-first century. Philip Jenkins in *The Next Christendom* predicts that by the year 2050 the majority of Christians will be people of color living primarily in the Southern Hemisphere.[1] Christianity is turning brown and moving south. Some North American blacks, unmindful of the movement of the larger Christian church, think that the future of preaching lies with conservative white churches with their conservative theology and the massive numbers of people they are able to draw on Sunday mornings. But the future of Christianity lies with the colored people of the world who will be living primarily in the global South. They will be the Christian majority, and they will set the theological agenda.

From all indications, the colored preaching of the future will be quite different from the traditional preaching of the West and more particularly the preaching of white, Western males. Although white males continue to set the homiletic agenda in American preaching circles, from all indications their ways of preaching and their ways of thinking through the foundational components of preaching are already being viewed as narrow, confining, and in some instances out of touch with the preaching done by people of color in the Southern Hemisphere. The kind of preaching with which we must concern ourselves and the homiletic theory that must guide it no longer lie in the white Western world of Europe or North America. As Christianity moves southward, the preaching of the twenty-first century will be comparably changed by immersion in the prevailing cultures of Africa, Latin America, and Asia.[2] This reality concerning the growth of the Christian church in the global South has shaped my interest in my ongoing search for distinctions in black preaching. The distinctive quest in the future will not be so much in black preaching but must now be broadened to include colored preaching.

For over a decade now, I have been involved in this quest to discover distinctiveness in black preaching. In the late nineties I enumerated what I believed to be broad and widely accepted characteristics of this style of preaching: a high regard for Scripture, creative rhetoric, an unabashed display of emotion, and a certain license or freedom in the preaching moment. I argued for five realms or domains of black preaching that aided blacks in their efforts to preach the whole counsel of God. I also argued, in equal measure, for a distinctive hermeneutic in black sermons, a template, if you will, that viewed God as a powerful agent proactively involved in the lives of the marginalized and the oppressed.[3]

I see my move into the broader sphere of colored preaching as a continuation of that work. The distinctiveness I have previously tried to describe has been primarily in comparison to the preaching of the white Protestant majority in the United States. Initially I engaged in this quest because I thought black preaching was being overlooked by those who were doing the research, writing, and publishing on the practice of preaching in the United States. As a student at Princeton Theological Seminary I remember reading book after book on preaching where black preachers were not mentioned or only slightly mentioned in passing. But as I have pointed out in previous publications,[4] there are works out there now written by people who are not black that make an effort to take the black preaching craft seriously: Richard Lischer, *The Preacher King*; Keith Miller, *Voice of Deliverance;* L. Susan Bond, *Contemporary African American Preaching*; O. C. Edwards, *A History of Preaching;* Paul S. Wilson, *The Four Pages of the Sermon;* and Gary Selby, *Martin Luther King and the Rhetoric of Freedom*, just to name a few.[5] In other instances blacks and whites have teamed up with one another and published the results of what they learned from each other's preaching tradition. Among those works are E. K. Bailey and Warren Wiersbe's *Preaching in Black and White;* Brian Blount and Gary Charles's *Preaching*

Mark in Two Voices; and Evans Crawford and Thomas Troeger's *The Hum: Call and Response in African American Preaching.*[6]

And of course there are blacks who have written about preaching, and while not specifically naming black preaching in their titles, it was clear that they had brooded over and reflected on the topic out of an African American context that gave sustenance and shape to the development of their homiletic. Among those are Samuel DeWitt Proctor in *The Certain Sound of the Trumpet;* Gardner Taylor in *How Shall They Preach;* James Harris's *Preaching Liberation;* Frank Thomas's *They Like to Never Quit Praisin' God;* and James Forbes's *The Holy Spirit and Preaching.*[7]

When one broadens the search for distinctions from black preaching to *colored* preaching, an entirely new realm of possibilities comes into view. The most striking dimension that comes to the fore in this expansion is theological worldview. I am coming more and more to believe that theological worldview has a lot to do with distinctiveness in black preaching as well as colored preaching. Others before me have said this and said it better: If you really want to know what the black church thinks theologically, listen to its preaching. Our theology has always been more implicit than explicit. But if you listen intently to black preaching, you can get a sense of those subtle chords that buttress and bind this preaching tradition.

I have always believed that the black theological worldview was much broader than the worldview deemed acceptable by the widely accepted Enlightenment theology. Scholars who have written on the future shape of Christianity have been most helpful in moving my thinking along in this regard. Among them are Andrew Walls, the distinguished European missiologist.

In a recent study titled "Christian Scholarship and the Demographic Transformation of the Church," Walls notes what he terms the most remarkable feature of Christian history in the twentieth century: the massive demographic and cultural shift in the composition of the Christian church.[8] Europe, says Walls, is no longer a Christian heartland, and North America is becoming subject to the same pressures. By the end of the twenty-first century two-thirds of the world's Christians may be living in the southern continents. Africa, Latin America, and some parts of Asia have now become the Christian heartlands. While the demographics of the Christian church have shifted southward, the thought processes and cultural awareness have not yet moved proportionately. Interesting![9]

Walls, of course, is not the first to note that Christianity is in decline in Western countries and that in Europe it dwindled out of recognition in the latter half of the twentieth century. Philip Jenkins in *The Next Christendom,* John Mbiti, and Kwame Bediako are among many who have made note of this demographic shift.[10] But what is quite interesting about Walls's essay and more directly related to my concern about the future shape of black preaching is what Walls believes will be the result of this shift in the twenty-first century and beyond:

> The implication is that Africa and Asia and Latin America and the Pacific seem set to be the principal theatres of Christian activity in its latest phase. What happens there will determine what the Christianity of the twenty-first and twenty-second centuries will be like. What happens in Europe and even in North America will matter less and less. It is Africans and Asians and Latin Americans who will be the *representative* Christians: those who represent the Christian norm, the Christian mainstream of the twenty-first and twenty-second centuries.[11]

I maintain that the black church in its present state bears some resemblance to this church of the future. Walls, Jenkins, Harvey Cox in *Fire From Heaven,*[12] and others have noted some of the belief patterns of Christians in the Southern Hemisphere, and some of them are not unlike the belief patterns of blacks in America. Even though ridiculed in some circles for being pre-critical in their understandings of the Bible, many American blacks never gave up their belief in the supernatural, miracles, and healings. In his brief essay, Walls focuses on African beliefs and isolates one task as illustrative of this larger theological undertaking to which he is calling the present generation of scholars: rethinking the framework of theology. By way of an example that could in no way be considered exhaustive of the rethinking Walls is calling for, Walls contrasts the African worldview with the Enlightenment worldview expounded by the missionaries who brought the gospel to Africa. Walls notes that fundamental to the Enlightenment worldview was a demarcated frontier between the empirical world—the world of what we can see and touch, the realm in which "repeatability" can reasonably be looked for—and the other world, the world of spirit. In the Enlightenment worldview, the natural could and must be distinguished from the supernatural. The non-Christian and anti-Christian wing of the Enlightenment argued that there was nothing on the other side of the frontier of the empirical world, or, if there was, we could know nothing about it. According to Walls, the greater part of the Western secular academy now works on that assumption, though it does not always make the assumption clear. It brackets out the whole of the "other" world, the world of spirit, even in the study of religion.[13]

But African visions of the world were different. The frontier between the empirical world and the spiritual world was being crossed and recrossed every day in both directions. Africans responded to the gospel in multitudes, but they could not easily lose the vision of that open frontier. As a result, the theology they inherited and the church practice based on it frequently did not seem to fit the facts of daily African experience. The problem, says Walls, is that Western theology is pared-down theology, cut and shaved to fit a small-scale universe. Most Africans, even when they were participating in Enlightenment activities, lived in a larger universe where the frontier was still open. That open frontier that Africans cross and recross daily is what I find helpful for the study of black preaching.[14]

I want to be specific in what I'm arguing here. I am arguing for the open frontier of the world of spirit, where boundaries are crossed and recrossed every day in both directions. I am not arguing that blacks view that world in the same way as their African brothers and sisters. I am arguing, however, that the pared-down theology of the white Western academy that was cut and shaved to fit a small-scale universe was always a tight fit for the theological world of the black church. Consequently, in a fashion similar to their African counterparts, the theology African Americans inherited and the church practices based on it did not seem to fit the facts of daily African American experience. There are similarities in worldviews between African Americans and Africans regarding the empirical world and spirit world. American blacks, in a manner similar to their African counterparts, even while accepting of many of the findings of the Enlightenment, cross and recross those boundaries each and every day. And those crossings are reflected in their preaching.[15]

The spirit world is much more a part of black lives and black religious experience than many people in the majority culture realize. There are things that blacks continue to believe about the spirit world that defy the Enlightenment requirement that says that which is real is only that which one can see, feel, and touch. Much to the chagrin of the Enlightened world, many in the black church never stopped believing in miracles, healing, the supernatural, and other such phenomena. Their theological worldview was much broader than the circumscribed worldview of the Enlightenment. And if you listen, you can hear this in black preaching, even to this day.

The world of spirit, as Walls suggests in his brief overview of African theology, must not be dismissed out of hand. Africans and African Americans still take that world seriously. There is some deep preaching to be found in the crossing of those boundaries between the empirical world and the world of spirit. Preachers cannot get all of their sermons from biblical commentaries or life experiences. Some parts of the sermon must come from those deep places of unseen reality. Those imaginative insights that come to you while preparing for preaching and even while you are up preaching don't always come from the usual places. They don't always come from one's knowledge of Scripture or one's understanding of theology. Neither do they come merely from one's familiarity with the richness of human experience both lived and observed. Sometimes those insights into preaching come only from divine initiative—where one crosses over into unseen reality.

Our task, first of all, is to own up to our continued belief in the world of spirit—that world on the other side of the frontier of the empirical world. We don't have to be ashamed of a tradition that crosses and recrosses that boundary on a regular basis. It is where African Americans have historically and traditionally communed with the divine. We must probe those depths as best we can for the theological and imaginative insights that they bring to our understanding of the holy and to our preaching. Blacks cross these boundaries all the time. One can hear it in their call stories and in their confessional preaching. William H. Myers, discussing the call experience of African American preachers, notes that voices heard by the callees are the sign that appears most frequently in the parts of the story that discuss the call experience itself. They occur in a variety of forms. However, the callees speak with absolute certainty and consistency about some aspect of the voices—that they heard a voice, that they heard what it said, and that they know when they heard it.[16] Something or someone beyond them is speaking to them in some manner.

When asked about his sermon preparation method, the renowned African American preacher Gardner Taylor speaks of entering that world without directly attributing it to the divine:

> I would want to think that a sermon idea has been decided for me, rather than I just decided it. I think that goes into that brooding. I shy away from the notion that it is all self-generated. And here we come upon the inexplicable. I was talking with Albert Einstein one morning in Princeton, and he said during the course of our conversation that an idea came to him. . . . We cannot know what he meant, but I think he meant something like what happens to all of us—that you are thinking about brooding and then something comes. Now is that self-generated? I don't think so. Maybe a part of it rises out of us, but a part of it comes down upon us. It's not just a matter of me deciding, and that is the mystery of it.[17]

A belief that we are in direct contact with God through the world of spirit—the unseen world of inner reality—infuses much of black preaching. This understanding guides and directs us in our beliefs and practices, and it also undergirds and enhances our preaching. Take the example of Martin Luther King Jr. during the early days of his leadership of the Montgomery bus boycott. Late one night King received a threatening telephone call. The unidentified voice on the other end warned King that he would soon be sorry for stirring up trouble in Montgomery. King said,

> I got out of bed and began to walk the floor. Finally, I went to the kitchen and heated a pot of coffee. I was ready to give up. I tried to think of a way to move out of the picture without appearing to be a coward. In this state of exhaustion, when my courage had almost gone, I determined to take my problem to God. . . . At that moment I experienced the presence of the Divine as I had never before experienced him. It seemed as though I could hear the quiet assurance of an inner voice, saying, "Stand up for righteousness, stand up for truth. God will be at your side forever." Almost at once my

fears began to pass from me. My uncertainty disappeared. I was
ready to face anything. The outer situation remained the same, but
God had given me inner calm.[18]

King makes contact with the divine—an unseen inner reality—
and it strengthens his resolve for the rest of his life. Yes, even to the
end of his life. Some would say, Ah, nothing more than a subjective
experience from a fearful preacher. But many of us believe King
made contact with the divine.

I hasten to add my own experience with unseen reality. Thirty-six
years ago I sensed the call to Christian ministry as a nineteen-year-
old boy in south Texas. I gathered my family together in the living
room of our home to tell them of my call experience. As I began to
speak to them, the phone rang. It was a woman who worked at the
hospital with my mother. She said, "Mrs. LaRue, I hate to bother you,
but I had a dream last night that won't go away. I dreamed your son
was called to preach, and I saw him standing in a room with people
gathered around him, and he was trying to tell you what the Lord had
done in his life." My mother said to the woman, "I will have to call
you back because that is exactly what he is doing right now."

We have always known there is more to the preaching life than the
realities of the empirical world that we can see and touch. We have
always known there is more to preaching than interpretive strategies
and correct biblical exegesis. In dealing with mystery there are other
dimensions that simply cannot be accounted for even when you have
followed every step of the exegesis process. Still we must wait for
God to speak. You must wait even after you have decided on a text.
Even when you cut it appropriately in order to focus your preaching. Even when you go all out to make sure they understand every
word in the passage. Even when you look to see what's around it,
what came before it, and what came afterward; who's speaking and
who is being addressed. Even when you consider the genre of the
passage—narrative, parable, epistle, song, prayer, and so forth—still
you know there is more. Even when you engage in brainstorming,
where you ask every conceivable question of the text before you,
there is more. Even when you put yourself in conversation with the
scholars through your reading of devotional and critical commentaries, there is more. Still there is this asking after God that must come

before the sermon is complete. When and where will God speak to me? When shall God's Spirit come down upon me? Come over me? When and where will God speak? Blacks, in similar fashion to their African brothers and sisters, have been more willing than most in North America to cross that divide between what is seen and unseen, between what can be known through investigation and discovery and what can be grasped only as gift and grace. It adds a dimension to our preaching that those laboring under the influence of the Enlightenment are all too inclined to resist.

Whether he is right or wrong, Andrew Walls notes that Africa's advancement and phenomenal growth may be due in large part to its distance from the Enlightenment. I urge blacks to struggle with both—the finds of the Enlightenment world and the realities of the unseen world. We have to move into that unseen reality. So many blacks are conscious of it, and more and more are willing to speak openly about it. It has an impact on our preaching, and it ties us to the broader world of colored preaching, and more importantly, to the future shape of preaching. In the creative process we have to be open to this larger theological worldview. We also have to be open to safeguards to keep it from going awry, but our search for safeguards must not diminish our search for the inner realities of the unseen world. Many of us have testimonies where we have had contact with phenomena from the spirit world. Whereas we have been hesitant to speak of these things, we could well be at home in the world of Andrew Walls's representative Christians of the twenty-first century. Our future is with the brown people of the world. Together we must forge a homiletic that more clearly represents the New Christians.

Chapter 5

African American Preaching and the Bible

*T*aking a text from a passage of Scripture and announcing a sermon title when preparing to preach continue to be the two clearest signals a preacher can send to a black congregation that he or she understands the importance of the primacy of the Word. Black congregants, by and large, go to church to hear the preacher expound on the written Word, and they don't really get a feel for the sermon until they hear the Scriptures or sense some connection between the Scriptures and what the preacher is saying.

Thus, black preaching is inextricably tied to Scripture. In the eyes of the black church a preacher without Scripture is like a doctor without a black bag, which is to say, what one needs to get the preaching job done comes with some kind of encounter with Scripture. Any preacher who seeks to be heard on a regular basis in a black church must learn some method of engaging the scriptural text and drawing from that encounter some sense of the Word of God revealed *to* and acting *on* the present-day human situation of the black listeners. Effective preachers recognize that this daunting task of creatively engaging Scripture and lived experience is at the center of their weekly preparation. Therefore the preacher must be familiar with the Bible. It is a well-worn saying that continues to hold true in the black church: Whatever they say about you, don't let it be said that you can't preach. The in-depth knowledge of Scripture required of the preacher cannot simply be a task-oriented familiarity with Scripture, for the Bible does not fully yield its treasures as the Word of God to those who visit it from time to time when fishing for a sermon. One has to live with the Scriptures and walk up and down the streets of the texts in order to have those texts speak forth with power and conviction.

It is both unwise and inaccurate to speak of a single way in which African Americans preach from the Scriptures in their quest for God. The danger lies in any claim to singleness of expression that purports to speak for an entire group of people with a four-hundred-year history on American soil. African Americans are quite diverse and complex in their makeup, in their religious beliefs and practices, and most certainly in their construal and use of the Scriptures. Black preaching and teaching are of necessity multifarious in their depths and expressions. Therefore, any attempt to outline the broad parameters of an African American use of the Bible must be qualified with words like *nonmonolithic*, *multifaceted*, and *diverse*. Such words help to remind us that every rule has an exception and no group can ever be said to do any one thing a certain way.

The Four Essentials of Preaching the Scriptures

There are four essentials that come together in the best of black preaching. They are God, the Scriptures, the preacher, and black lived experience. In a figure/ground relationship that is dynamic in its origin, these rudimentary components interact with one another in a manner that is most difficult to dissect and set apart, even for the purpose of establishing a framework for study. Yet these four essentials are at the heart of the black construal and use of the Bible, and they aid blacks in their quest to know what God has done *for* us and, of equal measure, what God requires *of* us. On the basis of these four fundamentals, blacks bring certain expectations to the preaching moment. First, when the Scriptures are being proclaimed, blacks believe that they are being addressed by God. Second, they expect that this address will come through the preacher of the Word after the preacher has faithfully explicated the text and sought in meaningful and relevant ways to wed that text to the lived experience of the black congregation.

God

At the heart of the black search of the Scriptures has been an unceasing quest for God and the things of God. Unlike many who claim a deep-seated love for the Bible, blacks have typically not made the mistake of worshiping the Bible. They have, however, sought in their preaching and teaching to probe the unsearchable riches of God's grace as they are witnessed to and attested in the Bible. So intense has been the black search for a divine encounter with God that in their early history in America, some former slaves were said to value their *experience* of God's power as the norm of Christian truth rather than the Bible itself.[1] In contemporary times, the Bible's importance for a large number of African Americans has been more functional than revelatory. That is, while blacks view the Bible as the primary way for them to encounter God, it is the way the Scriptures function, the way they are construed in black religion, that is of the utmost importance for blacks. In its functional import, the Bible does much more than simply witness to God's past acts on behalf of others; it actually speaks to blacks about who God is today and how God effects God's will and purpose in their present situations in life.

There is in black preaching a predominant interpretive strategy that shows up time and time again when one examines historical and present-day black uses of Scripture. That biblical hermeneutic concerns itself with God and God's actions especially as they are most fully and finally manifested in Jesus Christ. Blacks are by and large convinced that God is for them. They have historically believed the acts of God to be favorable and intentional on behalf of all those who, like themselves, have been marginalized and oppressed, neglected and looked over. Blacks believe God has continually championed their cause in spite of those who sought to relegate them to an inferior standing unworthy of the full force of God's providential care and concern. To this day, even among upwardly mobile blacks who consider that they have moved further in from the periphery of marginalization, some understanding of a God who is at work on their behalf continues to govern their construal of Scripture. While in some black circles this understanding has taken a selfish, narcissistic turn, it is nonetheless a dimension of the interpretive strategy blacks have employed. Blacks believe that God is for them—even when being for them is understood in a provincial, restrictive, and selfish manner. It is this template that governs their explication of Scripture.

It is not by accident that a popular refrain, mantra even, among the black religious public is, "God is good all the time; all the time God is good!" Blacks truly believe this about God. The God of power and might is good to them and good for them. Even when a particular text could conceivably be interpreted to the contrary, blacks do not despair, gloss over, or misread; they simply turn their view to the grand sweep of their eschatological hope, which is to say, they look to God's overall performance and promises in human history. That grand view of God, which has stood the test of time, grounds them in both their backward look and their forward glance (what God has done and what God has promised). The interpretive strategy that blacks employ allows them to say with confidence to any and all who doubt their understanding of God, "Come see what great things the LORD has done!" (based on Mk. 5:19).

A central truth blacks quickly came to embrace when they were allowed to read and interpret for themselves is that Scripture revealed a God of infinite power who could be trusted to act on their behalf. Historically blacks embraced the Christian God in large numbers only after they were able to make a connection between God's power and their servile situation in life. This direct relationship between black struggle and divine rescue colors the theological perceptions and themes of black preaching in a very decisive manner.[2]

A God who is unquestionably for them is what blacks see when they go to the Scriptures. Thus a distinctive characteristic of black preaching is that it testifies to that which blacks believe Scripture reveals about the sovereign God's involvement in the everyday affairs and circumstances of their existence. African Americans believe the sovereign God acts in very concrete and practical ways in matters pertaining to their survival, deliverance, advancement, prosperity, and overall well-being. This is not to suggest that God is at work only for blacks, but it is to say with power and conviction that blacks have not been left out of the redemptive purposes of almighty God.[3] This is what blacks see when they open the pages of the written Word of God.

The Scriptures

There is in black preaching a high regard for Scripture. Black preaching has historically been noted for its strong biblical content. In many black churches, biblical preaching, defined as preaching that allows a text from the Bible to serve as the leading force in shaping the content and purpose of the sermon, is the type of preaching considered to be most faithful to traditional understandings of the proclaimed Word.

Indeed, it is no secret that the Bible occupies a central place in the religious life of black Americans. More than a mere source for texts, it is the single most important source of language, imagery, and story for the black sermon. Though biblical literacy in black churches is greatly diminished from earlier years, it has yet to reach the state where the Bible's primacy as a rich resource for black preaching is no longer the case.

A noted white homiletician recently found it comical that blacks still draw many of their examples and illustrations in preaching directly from the Bible. He wanted blacks to broaden their reading circle to include examples and illustrations from literature and modern-day life. While I agree that the reading circle should be broadened, I do not agree that it should come at the expense of our love and high regard for the Bible and our continuing ability to find examples of our lives therein. The Scriptures still matter in black preaching. They are our guide and source to life as it is meant to be lived before God. One is hard-pressed to make his or her case in a black pulpit if the congregation comes to believe that the Scriptures do not have primacy.

Blacks, like other interpreters of the Bible, rarely operate with an explicitly formulated theory of the text. Yet their theoretical assumptions are undeniably present. The black belief that they are being addressed by God in the preaching of the Word is the foremost theoretical assumption in their construal of the Scriptures. This understanding of Scripture has been characterized as the *divine oracle paradigm*.[4] Several basic principles inform this paradigm. First, there is the conviction that the Bible constitutes one single genre. In the view of many blacks, while the Bible is composed of diverse materials, when properly arranged as a completed collection, it is seen as unfolding a single, continuous, coherent story of salvation history.[5] Second, God is believed to be the author of Scripture, which is to say, the Scriptures were written by numerous authors speaking in some direct sense on behalf of God. Thus, by extension, God may be viewed as the real author. Without apology, large numbers of blacks continue to believe this about the Scriptures. An often-cited passage is 2 Timothy 3:16–17: "All scripture is inspired by God and is useful for teaching, for reproof, for correction, and for training in righteousness, so that everyone who belongs to God may be proficient, equipped for every good work."

Third, there is a uniformity of revelation. If the black Bible is assumed to be a unified, coherent collection of writings that directly derive from God, it naturally flows that God is speaking in all its parts. In any given verse we can hear God's voice, and we can expect it to resonate with all the other parts to some degree. The idea that certain parts can be cast aside and treated as something less than God's word is anathema to large circles of blacks. A harmonious thread runs throughout the whole of Scripture and while some passages may be a bit distant from that melody, they are a part of God's overall song.[6]

Fourth, Scripture is directly expressive of divine will. This principle presupposes a direct correspondence between Scripture and divine intent and assumes that the will of God is somehow embodied within and expressed by the text. The text becomes the primary focus of the interpreter's attention and the primary locus of revelation. The place the preacher looks for or listens to the word of God is within the sacred pages of the Bible. Blacks believe that the attentive interpreter can hear God speaking directly through the text. So often in black preaching there will be little distance between the preacher and the events of the text. It's not uncommon to hear the preacher proclaim, "I heard Paul say the other day. . ." as if the preacher and Paul had recently been in conversation, for the preacher believes that God is speaking in the hear and now directly through the text.[7]

Blacks are often not given credit for the nuancing they do in this paradigm. To say that one expects to be addressed by God through Scripture is not to suggest that Scripture must be taken literally in all its parts. Instead, the search that drives the desire to understand and interpret the Scriptures grows out of the belief that somehow, in some manner, God is speaking through a particular text. The finds of historical-critical research are of immense benefit to blacks in their quest to hear the voice of God. Blacks simply refuse to relegate that voice strictly to the historical past.

The Preacher

Without question, the black preacher has been at the center of defining the black religious experience as it has existed in this country since its inception in the seventeenth century. Early on the black preacher took the lead in refashioning the Christian gospel in ways that made it contextually relevant to those who hungered to hear the gospel proclaimed in an idiom they could understand.

The exact time and place of the black preacher's origin in this country is difficult to determine. We do know that beginning in the late eighteenth and early nineteenth centuries southern evangelicalism gave rise to large numbers of black preachers who exhorted and preached without the requirements of formal training. Albert Raboteau and Nathan Hatch are among those who have documented the appeal of southern evangelicalism's more informal approach to religion.

Hatch cites three obvious reasons that blacks, slave and free, swarmed into Methodist and Baptist folds, spurning the high-church traditions. First, early Baptists and Methodists earned the right to be heard. They welcomed African Americans as full participants in their communions and condemned the institution of slavery—though we all know there was an eventual retreat on these issues by white Baptist and Methodist brethren. The second reason for the enormous influx of black converts into the Methodist and Baptist camps is that these groups proclaimed a Christianity that was fresh and capable of being readily understood and immediately experienced. The third and most important reason for the great influx, however, was the emergence of black preachers and exhorters. Blacks for the first time were granted the right and the responsibility of openly and publicly interpreting Scripture for themselves. That hard-won right to interpret and to proclaim has never been relinquished by blacks. Then and now, in black preaching the text matters. The surge of African Americans into the Christian faith between the Revolution and the

War of 1812 paralleled the decisive rise of the black preacher. Virtually unknown in colonial America, black preaching exploded in the experimental climate generated by passionate Baptist and Methodist evangelicals.[8]

By the 1830s most southern evangelicals had thoroughly repudiated a heritage that valued blacks as fellow church members. Pushed to the fringes of white churches, African American preachers asserted the autonomy of black Christianity overtly and in secret. What preserved the black church as the first public institution over which blacks had control was nothing but the courage, foresight, and determination of the black preacher.[9]

Blacks continue to attach great importance to the one who proclaims the message. Any ole individual will not do. The person up before them must have been called by God from the midst of the congregation to stand and proclaim the word of God. Blacks have never been huge fans of preaching roundtables or conversational preaching. The sermon is not simply information being disseminated by a people-friendly individual who by some luck of the draw happens to be up before them on any given morning. The person who stands to preach is not there because it is his or her *turn*. Rather, preachers stand to preach because it is their *time*—a time that has been set and ordered by God. The one who stands before the congregation has been called by God and selected by the congregation to perform this task each Sunday. This is one of the primary reasons the black preacher continues to be held in such high esteem in many church circles. Black preachers are still considered to be God's anointed, who bring to the waiting congregation the word from God. The genre of the selected or assigned text notwithstanding—narrative, epistle, or apocalyptic—the expectation among the listening congregation is the same: they expect to be addressed by God when the preacher stands to preach the gospel.

Black Lived Experience

Fourth, the preacher must make a connection between the God who acts in Scripture and the God who acts in their present-day life. Some refer to this dynamic as concretizing the gospel. In the call-and-response that is so much a part of traditional black preaching one can hear a congregant shout out and say, "Make it plain, preacher!" In other words, make that connection between the God of the Scriptures and the God who is at work in my life this day. The connection does not always have to be explicit, and in many instances the listening congregation can make their own connection if the preacher is sufficiently skilled in painting the picture.

When examining the structure of a traditional black sermon, one can see that its initial formation comes to life through reflecting on the common life experiences of the people of faith. Consequently a sermon is best heard when it offers an insightful perspective on lived experience as opposed to the mere enunciation of theological formulations that tend to be abstract and devoid of the human touch. For this reason an understanding of "situations," or domains of experience, and how to name them and build on them is crucial in the development of the black sermon.

A domain is a sphere or realm that covers a broad but specified area of black experience and also provides a category for sermonic reflection, creation, and organization. Domains are based on and grow out of long-standing beliefs and experiences in black secular and religious life. An awareness of these broad areas is immensely important for understanding how Scripture and black experience come together in the preaching moment.

The five broad domains of experience that appear often enough in black life and preaching to constitute a pattern are personal piety, care of the soul, social justice, corporate concerns, and maintenance of the institutional church.[10]

Personal Piety

The first and most common domain that reflects black experience and provides a framework for the creation and organization of the black sermon is personal piety. Pietism emphasizes "heart religion," the centrality of the Bible for faith and life, the royal priesthood of the laity, and strict morality. The black attraction to personal piety can be traced in this country to the evangelical revivalism that swept America in the late eighteenth and early nineteenth centuries. In this era of religious fervor the evangelicals' demands for clean hearts and righteous personal lives became the hallmarks of African American religion in the South.

The more narrow understanding of personal piety that concerns itself with faith and personal formation is the dimension that has had and continues to have the greatest impact on black preaching. A large number of contemporary blacks experience life in this broad domain. It emphasizes prayer, personal discipline, moral conduct, and the maintenance of a right relationship with God. Many are convinced they have not heard the gospel if it does not address some aspect of life as it is lived in this domain. Even ministers who are known for their active participation on the social justice front preach sermons from time to time that have as their central focus some matter related to personal piety.[11]

Care of the Soul

The second domain of experience (i.e., belief and practice) on which black preaching reflects and to which it is directed may be characterized as "care of the soul." Care of the soul describes that area of experience that focuses on the well-being of individuals. It is, however, more than mere comfort for the bereaved, forgiveness for the guilty, and help for the sick and needy; it is preeminently the renewal of life in the image of Christ. Thus it has as its purpose not only the giving of comfort but also the redirection of life. The preaching that grows out of reflection on this domain concerns itself with the healing, sustaining, guiding, and reconciling of persons as they face the changes and challenges of common human experiences—experiences that are exacerbated in black life through systemic and capricious discrimination and prejudice.

Preaching that centers on experiences in need of healing aims to overcome some impairment by restoring people to wholeness and by leading them to advance beyond their previous conditions. Sustaining seeks to help persons overcome an overwhelming sense of loss. Guiding helps them determine what they ought to do when they are faced with a difficult problem wherein they must choose between various courses of thought or action, and reconciliation helps alienated persons to establish or renew proper and fruitful relationships with God, family, significant others, friends, and neighbors. The function of sermons created out of reflection on this domain is to salve or heal the wounds and brokenness of life through some form of encouragement, exhortation, consolation, renewal, instruction, or admonishment.[12]

Social Justice

The third domain centers on social justice. Matters pertaining to racism, sexism, ageism, and other forms of discrimination fall under the scope of this particular domain. Social justice is defined as a basic value and desired goal in democratic societies that includes equitable and fair access to institutions, laws, resources, and opportunities without arbitrary limitations based on age, gender, national origin, religion, or sexual orientation. Racial justice, defined as equal treatment of the races, has been the most prominent component of the social justice domain in black experience. Discrimination and prejudice are the twin evils the black preacher has spoken out against most vociferously since the inception of the black church.

Those who preach out of this domain view God as the source of social justice and are absolutely certain that God's power is on their side in their quest for social reform. They do not seek necessarily to overthrow the societal system per se but to reform it so that it conforms once again to fundamental principles of fairness and equality. Their preaching aims at constructive social change. Consequently, God's power is believed to be made available in the present order to bring about fair and just treatment in systems and structures that negatively impact all people, including blacks.[13]

Corporate Concerns

The fourth domain concerns itself with corporate concerns. Preaching that grows out of reflection on this domain recognizes that there are in black life certain issues and interests that arise out of its unique history and cultural experiences in this country. Because such matters are believed to pertain uniquely to blacks, many believe they are best addressed by blacks. Inasmuch as this domain has at its center matters that pertain specifically to blacks, it tends more toward exhortations of self-help, uplift, and racial solidarity.

While it often concerns matters of social justice for black people, it is not confined to social justice. Its primary distinction is that it speaks to matters that particularly and peculiarly affect black life. Unlike the domain of social justice, which seeks the common good of all, the domain of corporate concerns is specifically geared to black interests.

Matters of vital importance in black life are thought by many to be best dealt with by other blacks. Examples include teenaged pregnancy, exhortations to blacks to lift themselves from the welfare rolls, black-on-black crime, calls for educational excellence, and so forth. These are the kinds of things that can best be said to blacks by other blacks. More pointedly, there are some things that should only be said to blacks by other blacks. Issues and concerns that fall within this realm have historically been addressed from black pulpits.

Maintenance of the Institutional Church

The fifth domain, maintenance of the institutional church, is vastly important to the ecclesiastical life of the faith community as an institution. Since it is more concerned with ethos than specific acts, it operates at a higher level of abstraction and is more inclined to be coupled with one or more domains in a sermon. Owing to the historical importance of the black church in the African American community, blacks by and large experience "church" not simply as a place to attend worship but as a way of life. Church is more than a once-a-week encounter; it is an affirming presence that shapes and molds self-understanding, self-worth, behavior, and lifestyle. For this reason, African Americans tend to identify more strongly with a denomination, a specific fellowship, and a specific location than their counterparts in the majority culture.

Sermons in this domain reflect on the work of the people as a gathered fellowship, thus the teachings of the faith with respect to discipleship, missions, evangelism, Christian education, benevolence, and so on, usually find expression in this realm. Sermons that speak to the promotion, building, and upkeep of the physical plant are also common. How members are to behave and interact with one another and the requirements for spiritual growth and maturity within the church's many departments and auxiliaries are also addressed. This, however, is more than stewardship preaching or catechetical indoctrination; it is preaching that gives continued life and sustenance to the institutional church, which in turn reaffirms and upholds its participants.

In that these domains represent ideal types, it is seldom the case that any one sermon is purely of one particular domain in the strictest sense of the term. In fact, it is quite possible for a given sermon to have some characteristics from more than one of the domains cited. The overall focus of the sermon, the primary situation in life to which it is addressed, and the makeup of the intended listeners will ultimately determine the domain that most fittingly characterizes the sermon. Text and lived experience as outlined in the aforementioned five domains of experience are brought together and held in tension in the best of black preaching. The preacher skillfully employs both in the structuring of a sermon, which must have at its central core some understanding of who God is and where God is at work in the world today. Over time a balanced approach to preaching out of these five domains will provide a congregation with a steady diet of preaching that is both enlightening and transformative. The five domains allow for a holistic approach to preaching because they take both the individual and corporate dimensions of human existence into account.[14]

Chapter 6

Imagination and the Exegetical Exercise

*A*n enduring criticism of American Protestant preaching, and especially the preaching of the mainline churches, is that on the whole it is too flat, too horizontal, too colorless—in a word, unimaginative.[1] It too often lacks sparkle, intrigue, provocative thought, and mental images that help us to see and to say the Word in new ways. The preaching that so many of us are inclined to do is discursive and rationalistic, given to simple outline form as if that's all our people expect from us. Our creative energy goes into saying it quickly and quietly, getting the gospel drudgery out of the way as soon as possible. More often than many of us would like to admit, we are, in a word, boring. We speak only because we *have to say something*, as opposed to speaking because we *have something to say*. Fred Craddock is right when he says, "It is unfortunate and unfair that imagination has been popularly allied primarily with fantasy and thus often spoken of pejoratively as 'just imagination' in the sense of the unreal and the untrue."[2]

Why is so much of our preaching lacking in imagination these days? Are we still reeling from the Dragnet effect of modernity—the facts ma'am, nothing but the facts?[3] Or do we share John Calvin's fear of pretty preaching and therefore simply embark on what many believe to be the unadorned, "plain style" preaching of the Reformed tradition?[4] It may well be that the things that preclude us from imaginative and creative preaching are legion. Yet the question will not go away: How can we employ the imagination more effectively in service to the sermon, to the preached Word, to the God who is for us, to the God who came among us in particularity—in history, in culture, in time and space—in the human flesh of a carpenter's son? What are we doing when we think imaginatively about the preached Word? Hopefully we are bringing to conscious formation new, interesting, and creative ways of presenting images and ideas that embody, shape, illumine, clarify, and render accessible the Word of God on a particular day to a particular people.

Imagination helps us to see and to say what often lies dormant within us. It is this seeing and saying that is so lacking in biblical exegesis for sermon preparation. Too often at our study table the poet is silenced by the technician in an effort to get the factual answers to those important exegetical questions: Where is the best place to cut this text? Do I clearly understand all of the words in the passage? What comes before and after the passage? What genre of Scripture is it? What is the theological center of the passage? And what is the sermonic focus for the listeners for today?

These are important questions indeed. Unfortunately, however, somewhere in between or, even worse, near the end of this necessary exercise, it dawns on the preacher that the imagination has not been an active participant in the process. Thus, rather belatedly the imagination is invited in, but only after the other more important questions are seated at the table. Therein lies the problem. Imagination is not simply a *step* in the exegetical process, nor is it an afterthought, an add-on, or a Johnny-come-lately gloss on a point in need of further clarification. Imagination is a process unto itself. It should permeate the whole of the exegetical exercise. It is the imagination that must envelop our exegesis and not the other way around. Sermon preparation at its best is shot through and through with imaginative insights and possibilities.

A fertile imagination will simply not wait its turn to contribute to the orderly, sequential exegetical exercise. Even though that exercise is foundational to effective preaching, it does not follow that it is the best way to evoke the imagination. Imagination is not static; it is dynamic. It does not have a "place" in the process; it permeates the entire exercise. It is present throughout. It does not even wait for the preacher to sit down at the study table to begin the formal investigation of the text. No! The imagination often beckons the preacher to the place of study. Before the preacher can even get to the study table, ideas, examples, slices of life, and anecdotes come hurtling forth like a bolt of lightning or an impatient baby making an early exit from the womb. This is why so many great ideas see the light of day on pieces of scrap paper, napkins, or the back of airline boarding passes. The imagination simply will not wait.

The only thing that should take precedence over openness to the imagination is our openness to the Spirit. And just as this openness to the movement of the Spirit cannot be assumed but rather eagerly sought and accepted on its own terms, so too, the imagination. The imagination will not be ordered around by any predetermined process. It is coauthor, not coeditor. It creates and calls forth. It does not merely review and rearrange. It is there throughout, impatiently insisting on a hearing. Imagination is at the crossroads of what Gardner Taylor calls that "mysterious romance between preparation and inspiration."[5] It involves a whimsical mixture of seeing and saying. Sometimes we can see it even when we can't say it. At other times it is vocalizing it that helps us better to see it. Its point of origination notwithstanding, it is not far from consciousness. Some experts on the inner workings of the brain maintain that humans use only about ten percent of their brain power. No truer words have been spoken when one considers the untapped potential and limitless possibilities of our imagination. Before, during, and after formal preparation for preaching, the imagination is there pushing, cajoling, pressing its case, speaking into the preacher's ear and trying to gain a hearing if only the technical will occasionally yield to the poetic. The preparation process needs both. At their best technician and poet are locked in a symbiotic relationship of creativity. During times of study this interchange forces itself on the preacher. At once the factual investigation is foremost only to defer and recede into the background as the poetic inference takes over. It is this all-important back-and-forth that helps the preacher to benefit most from the use of imagination in sermon preparation.

It is clear from contemporary preaching manuals that an effective use of the imagination is not uppermost in the minds of many homileticians. In one sense this is understandable, for the imagination so often defies categories, nomenclature, and rules of engagement. Some homileticians don't even mention it, as if it has no place in the more technique-oriented exercise of sermon preparation. Others seem to suggest that it has a place, just not a very important one.

Thus, for them, it simply shows up as something you think about at a certain place in the sermon preparation process. How can a process so vital to preaching be given such short shrift in so many preaching manuals?

In all too many "how-to" preaching books, when the imaginative process is mentioned, what is meant to flow freely too often shows up as just another step in the exegetical exercise. Thinking imaginatively is not some slow grinding process where you squeeze out some creative thought or idea after much laborious toil and heavy mental labor brought on by the step-by-step exegesis investigation. It does take some work to craft the fruits of imagination into formal speech, but that comes later when the sermon is set down in writing. But the fresh burst of naked imagination is different from the harvested fruits of imagination. Naked imagination at its best is a gift! It's like manna falling from heaven, where you freely receive what is being given, knowing all the time that it is coming in such grand and gracious proportions that you simply do not have the wherewithal to receive it in full. No sermon is big enough or long enough to contain all that comes to us as imaginative gift in preparation for preaching. The gift of naked imagination is answered prayer: Give us today what we need for today.

When the imagination is allowed to roam freely, your focus is on harnessing and harvesting what has been given and not on sweating and searching, trying to think up something new. Imagination at work looks more like a construction site rather than a ribbon-cutting ceremony at a grand opening. In its spontaneity it is more akin to the brash child in the classroom who answers out of turn—though correctly—as opposed to the timid child waiting patiently with hand in the air to be recognized. Imagination rushes past order. It is impatient with rules and regulations. Control freaks will always have difficulty with the quixotic emphasis inherent in imagination. There is undeniably disorder and disarray when imagination is roaming about the study table. But out of that disorder can spring forth ideas that would make the Athenians at the Areopagus proud, for what comes forth is the hearing and telling of something new.

Trying to harness the imagination through theoretical definitions alone is the best way to hinder it. I think one of the worst things you can write is a boring book on the imagination. It does such a disservice to this free flow of ideas. While there are any number of excellent writers who have thought through the theoretical implications of this process—Charles Rice, Thomas Troeger, and Paul Scott Wilson among them—theory alone will not unlock its treasures. Of course, one should read the theoretical books, but I also think it is all right to begin the process of thinking imaginatively simply by accepting the process as gift. By which I mean, instead of focusing so much on how it comes, focus instead on the given that it will come. When it comes to the imagination, it's perfectly acceptable to be what the business world calls an "unconscious competent"—a person who knows how to do something but is not necessarily able to explain it to others. In the words of the apostle Paul, our task is to stir up the gift that is in us. The power to imagine is within you. The power to think through a text and use your imagination to create a sermon is within you. To know the source of the imagination is no guarantee that you will be the beneficiary of its end results. Accept the gift, and practice harnessing its creativity.

Three Ways to Harness the Imagination

How do you organize what is already in you? And how do you harness these free-flowing streams of continuous imaginative thoughts? As previously mentioned, there is no one set place, no particular "step," no fitting moment for the imagination in the exegetical process. However, imagination received as gift can be bracketed around three different poles—initial, informed, and enhanced.

Initial Imaginative Thoughts

Initial imaginative thoughts are probably the closest things to the madness and sensual thoughts about which the early writers warned us. These are the first thoughts that come flowing from our innermost being. Sometimes these ideas flow from our lived experience before we even read a passage of Scripture. At such times it is experience in search of Scripture. At other times ideas flow when we reflect momentarily on a biblical passage as we remember it. Still at other times it is a fresh reading of and/or a sustained focus on Scripture that stirs the imagination. Something in experience or in Scripture pricks the imagination, and the flow begins in earnest.

Initial imaginative thoughts may best be described as "unadulterated eisegesis." To engage in this reading into Scripture one's own ideas takes pluck. Why? Because it takes resourceful courage and daring to think imaginatively and to dare to allow such thoughts to see the light of day. But the gains of such daring could well be worth the risk. Even though initial imaginative thoughts grow out of our ignorance, sinfulness, sensuality, prejudices, and preferences, they still have a place in the process. They get us going. They push us back from the jet bridge, enabling us to taxi down the runway for our imaginative flight. This is true with respect to Scripture and to life. Most exegetical exercises frown on eisegesis since this reading into Scripture is thought to do a great disservice to what the text actually means. Yet sometimes the most creative ideas happen just at this point of uninformed wonder. These initial, fleeting thoughts have a place in the process. I encourage preachers at least to entertain them and possibly even to jot them down whenever and wherever they arise.

Informed Imaginative Thoughts

Informed imaginative thoughts are the imaginative reflections that grow out of thinking about what is actually in Scripture. This is the time in the exegetical exercise where you put yourself in conversation with the scholars and bring the formal tools of study to bear on the process of discovering the meaning of the text. But here again, imagination should already be a part of the process. There should be no need to invite the imagination in. Although there are many good exegetical methods for helping preachers to gain a sense of the text and subsequently the claim of the text on the hearers,[6] you don't put your imagination on hold when you are in the process of actually gaining a hold on Scripture. I vehemently disagree with those who say informed reflection hinders the imaginative process. Informed reflection unleashes your imaginative potential. It is when you really begin to understand what is going on in a text that the imagination places before you unlimited ideas and ways of envisioning it. Again, you move back and forth, if not on paper, most assuredly in your mind, between informed insight and imaginative possibilities. Even when one is searching through Bible dictionaries, monographs, commentaries and so forth, the imagination is equally active in the search. Even if it's just an inkling of an insight, jot it down. Many of these fragmentary thoughts come to naught while others come to have a place of prominence in the creation of the sermon. There are so many "aha" moments when the preacher is deeply involved in getting at the meaning of a text. One can almost hear the rush and feel the excitement of the imagination at work. Experienced preachers have the ability to separate the imaginative wheat from the chaff in their heads. However, in the early years of their preaching preparation, inexperienced preachers should simply write them down as they move through their investigatory process.

Enhanced Imaginative Thoughts

The work of imagination is never done. Even when the sermon is as complete or as pulpit worthy as one has time to make it before the Sunday preaching hour, let the imagination continue to work. Don't be afraid to add to your prepared manuscript. A written manuscript does not a sermon make. The manuscript is but an arrested performance than can only be brought to life through the living voice. Feel free to drop those pearls of great price as the imagination continues to produce even after you stand to preach, for even as you preach the sermon is yet pregnant with imaginative possibilities. Temper it, of course, so that you don't go off on a tangent, but a sentence or two of insight that comes to you while preaching enhances the sermon and honors the imagination as it continues to work and place itself at the service of the preached word. Even after the sermon has been preached, and the imagination begins to look wistfully on the sermon as past event, ideas continue to come. Jot them down on the manuscript. At some point you'll have an opportunity to preach that sermon or that passage of Scripture again.

Imagination is akin to the Spirit in that it blows where it will. It comes upon us as a sudden burst of illumination and powerful insight that defies being tamed or confined by the precision and accuracy of the written and thus repeatable word. Imaginative construals are at once powerful and elusive, overbearing and fleeting. They come upon our mental horizon so forcefully that it is most difficult at times to jot down the faint glimmer of what just whisked past us with the speed of Halley's comet. Others quickly vanish into our mental sea of reason and respectability, while others in their haste must be consigned to certain death. In such cases one can only hope that they will resurrect themselves on a slower day at a slower pace.

Sources of Sermonic Ideas

There are at least four sources for sermonic ideas in every preacher. An awareness of sources is a good way to prime the pump of the imaginative process. The first source for sermonic ideas is the Scriptures. If sermonic ideas are going to come from Scripture, then it has to be assumed that one is fairly familiar with the Scriptures. All too many preachers are unfamiliar with Scripture today, or they have little or no sense of what they ought to be looking for in Scripture with respect to preaching. I once heard a colleague in homiletics say she found so little in Scripture that was relevant to her life. It is disturbing to hear any preacher make a comment like that and all the more disturbing when that preacher is also a homiletics professor. Bryant Kirkland, pastor for twenty-five years at the Fifth Avenue Presbyterian Church in New York City, used to hand the students in his preaching class a list of some three hundred biblical/theological themes and ideas right out of Scripture. Those themes concerned themselves with love, grace, sin, election, covenant, faith, hope, prayer, peace, the kingdom of God, sanctification, salvation, healing, family, grief, failure, stewardship, justice, discipleship, second chances, fellowship, and so forth. Scripture is an excellent way to get ideas for preaching.

A second source of ideas for the sermon comes from lived experience, that is, from the everyday events, happenings, and occurrences of life in which our encounters with the divine can be identified and named. I urge students to throw away their sermon illustration books and go about life observing and then naming the presence of God in the unfolding events of our everyday human existence. Some of these events are things that happen to us directly (personal), and others can be gained through listening or reading about the experiences of others (observed). Homileticians have different ideas about the use of stories, slices of life, and illustrations that come to us out of lived experience. Some say they should never be used in the pulpit, while others say they should be used in moderation. My own view is that moderation in all things should prevail. When an idea out of lived experience can shed light and bring illumination and greater understanding to the word then I think it is appropriate to use it. Some parameters are in order:

- They should not take on a life of their own
- Preachers should not make themselves the hero or heroine of the story
- One should never claim that an experience has happened to them when in fact it has not
- Others should not be named without first getting their permission and notifying them ahead of time what you intend to say.

Third, sermonic ideas can come from the depths of our despair. If one looks inward deeply enough, you can usually find what is common to the human predicament. In the deep places of our failures and fears, of our dashed hopes and shattered dreams, we can often find much that is common to the human situation. In the deep places of our grief and unresolved conflict, in those places where we return to struggle once again with our inner demons, we can find common ground with other human beings. I am not suggesting that preachers get up and preach about the deep places of our despair, but rather that we come to recognize those places and see how they help us to probe and understand what is common to all our struggles in the various situations of life. Gardner Taylor would often say to preachers that their preaching had no blood on it, meaning that what they preached about had little or no hint of struggle, pain, or difficulty in it. Too often preaching that never touches on the depths of human despair is too inclined to sound like the mere recitation of puppet sins and secondary utterances. In effective preaching I think there must be this probing and wrestling with the hard truths of our common existence.

Finally, sermonic ideas come from divine initiative. When all is said and done, some ideas just come to us out of the clear blue. People of faith are inclined to ascribe these ideas to God. I conducted a

Q&A with Gardner Taylor in *Power in the Pulpit*.[7] I asked Taylor how he went about preparing his sermons each week:

> **LaRue:** How do you move from an initial idea that comes to you to the finished sermon?
>
> **Taylor:** I would want to think that a sermon idea has been decided for me, rather than I just decided it. . . . Maybe part of it rises out of us, but part of it comes down upon us. It's not just a matter of me deciding, and that is the mystery of it.[8]

Taylor's point was that he clearly believed that an idea outside of and beyond him came to him. He quickly added that one must put oneself in a place and posture where such was more likely to happen. Clearly, he wanted something in his sermon preparation process from beyond him to speak to him. I call it divine initiative.

Granted, what I'm calling divine initiative could simply be the old bus, bath, and bed phenomenon. Garrett Green in *Imagining God* noted how important intellectual achievements appear to result from an abrupt reorganization of given materials, the result of which suddenly appears ready-made on the mental scene.[9] Such insights, he notes, quoting from gestalt theorist Wolfgang Kohler, characteristically occur at times of great passivity called the three Bs . . . the Bus, the Bath, and the Bed.[10] What I'm calling divine initiative could simply be the three Bs phenomenon. But it is the case that there are times when ideas come to us out of nowhere that help to move along our preaching intentions for the upcoming week. All these sources for sermon ideas are in service to a divine encounter. If the Scriptures don't point us toward God, then we've simply had a good time wandering around in Bible land. If the lived experiences—personal and observed—don't point us toward God, then we never get to the all important *so what* question. If the probe into the depths of our despair does not point us toward God, then parishioners will rightly come to feel that they have heard little, if any, good news. If divine initiative does not point us toward God, then to what end has this brilliant reorganization of materials come to life? All these ideas are in service to the divine encounter we seek to evoke between the sovereign God and his people. We are not simply passing out information but we are in search of a moment of illumination that leads to encounter, change, and transformation.

Chapter 7

Why Black Preachers Still Love Artful Language

America no longer values carefully wrought oral expression in the way that it did even in the recent past. . . . Modern America, then, is a country where rigorously polished language, of a sort only possible when channeled through the deliberate activity of writing, is considered insincere. . . . And it leaves us culturally and even intellectually deprived.
—*John McWhorter*[1]

One of the most notable characteristics of African American preach-·ing is the skillful use of oral language as a prized communicative tool. How best to convey the gospel through formal, crafted speech continues to be a studied and highly sought-after art among young and old black preachers alike. Contemporary linguists have noted with some alarm and sadness the loss of appreciation for rhetorical eloquence and great American oratory among typical Americans. John McWhorter attributes this loss to several things. First, he claims Americans have lost their love for their native language:

> To be a modern American is to lack a native love of one's language that is typical of most humans worldwide. . . . One often hears foreigners praising the beauty, the majesty, the richness of expression, of their native languages—both in and away from their homelands.[2]

Not so in America, according to McWhorter. Contemporary Americans do not love English. We do not celebrate it overtly, nor do we have anything to say about it if pressed on the point.[3] Second,

81

he attributes our loss of love for high language to the 1960s' main-streaming of the counterculture that discouraged the public celebration of our nation:

> Events in the sixties deeply transformed Americans' conventional wisdom regarding the legitimacy of their ruling class and the very concept of authority. . . . Before the 1960s, the conviction that the American experiment itself was fundamentally illegitimate was largely limited to certain political sects and intellectuals. After Vietnam and then Watergate, a less focused form of this senti-ment became a conventional wisdom among the educated, and proceeded to become a cultural zeitgeist. . . . The mainstreaming of the counterculture actually *predicts* that linguistically, every day would become Causal Day in America. . . . At such a cultural moment, formality becomes repressed, boring, unreflective, and even suspect, while Doing Your Own Thing is genuine, healthy, engaged and even urgent.[4]

Thus the new American tendency is to distrust forms of English to the extent that they stray from the way we use language while "doing our own thing" as we gab.

Third, McWhorter attributes our loss of love for language to our national shift from a written to an oral culture:

> A society that cherishes the spoken over the written . . . is one that marginalizes extended, reflective argument. Spoken language . . . is best suited to harboring easily processible chunks of informa-tion, broad lines, and emotion.[5]

At first glance, McWhorter seems to suggest that preference for spo-ken over written language has contributed to the loss of sustained, reflective thought, which can best be achieved through writing, thus undercutting my argument for blacks' ongoing appreciation for artful, oral speech. However, what McWhorter intends with the phrase "spoken language" is unadorned talk, casual talk that is the equivalent of "Whatever comes up comes out." Or as McWhorter says, "Just talking as opposed to speaking." It is this "unadorned speech" that McWhorter is referring to when he speaks of cherish-ing the spoken over the written. While it is true that there is indeed a heavy emphasis on orality in black preaching, black preachers are hardly engaging in "unadorned talk" in their oral presentations on Sunday morning. What you hear from black pulpits is a carefully crafted selection of words in which the preachers give the impression of spontaneity, pleasing the expectations of a listening congregation that prizes spontaneity as a sign of the movement of the Spirit. But in actuality, much thought and careful consideration have gone into the selection of each word, thought pattern, and argument that the black preacher speaks (or intends to speak). Thus when McWhorter speaks of a shift from a written culture to an oral culture as a cause of our lack of appreciation for artful rhetoric, he is speaking of America's preference for unadorned speech, not the well-crafted, oral presentation that is the end result of the black preacher's carefully honed words. It is America's preference for unadorned talk that has contributed to the decline of crafted speech, not the highly stylized oral speech of the black pulpit.

Fourth, McWhorter cites electric amplification as playing a role in the decline of artful language:

> Before the 1920s the public speaker had to reach a mass of hearers with the naked voice. This required high volume, which in turn favored a theatrical tone, majestic pacing, and planned phraseology. When speaking as loudly and clearly as possible one is less likely to insert hedges like "you know" and string phrases together in quick succession without considering their strict logical coherence. To wit, yelling discourages one from talking.[6]

This loss of the love of language—that is, the careful, reflective, precise speech of which McWhorter and other linguists write— cannot be said to have had the same corrosive effects in black culture and especially in black preaching. Many blacks continue not only to dress themselves in their Sunday best for the worship service but also to dress their English in its Sunday best.[7] The black church seems to be able to make a distinction between "grandiloquence" and "eloquence."

This ongoing love of language and the desire to put forth well-crafted speech can be found in a cross section of black preaching styles, educational levels notwithstanding. It can be found in Bruce Rosenberg's intellectual (manuscript) preachers with their formal training as well as in his spiritual preachers who believe themselves to

be totally dependent on God's guidance for what they say in the sermon.[8] This love of language can also be found in Albert Raboteau's
definition of black folk preaching or old-time country preaching, a
style of preaching he describes as a complex verbal art governed by
strict performance rules that require skill and dedication to master.[9]
The origin of the folk preacher dates back to the days of slavery.

Historically, oratorical ability and style are usually listed among
the reasons that the slave minister held such a unique position on the
plantation. Almost all writers who had a firsthand view of this old
type of religious leader point out the strange gift for elocution, which
seemed on the one hand to draw to him the less fortunate among the
slave population and, on the other, to offer to the white members
of the community an interesting spectacle in the way of religious
devotion, or a comic diversion for entertainment of guests.[10] Eugene
Genovese in *Roll Jordan Roll* argues that given the specific character
of their religion—its African soul and utter, slave-conditioned necessity for a plain message to the heart—the slaves naturally looked to
those who could understand and address themselves to their hopes
and misery.[11] Folk preachers often fulfilled this role.

The style of the folk sermon, which was shared by black and white
evangelicals alike, was built on a formulaic structure based on phrases,
verses, and whole passages the preacher knew by heart. Characterized by repetition, parallelisms, dramatic use of voice and gesture,
and a whole range of oratorical devices, the sermon began with normal conversational prose, then built to a rhythmic cadence, regularly
marked by the exclamations of the congregation, and climaxed in a
tonal change accompanied by shouting, singing, and ecstatic behavior. The preacher, who needed considerable skill to master this art,
acknowledged not his own craft but rather the power of the Spirit,
which struck him and set him on fire.[12] The dynamic pattern of call
and response between preacher and people was vital to the progres-
sion of the sermon, and unless the Spirit roused the congregation to
move and shout, the sermon was essentially unsuccessful.[13]

The oratorical skills of black women preachers were equally held
in high regard by listeners on the slave plantation. Lydia Maria Child,
the wife of a slave owner, recalled her experience of listening to the
powerful oratory of a Negro woman preacher:

Her description of the resurrection and the day of judgment must have been terrific to most of her audiences, and was highly exciting to me whose religious sympathies could never be roused by fear.[14]

The folk (or spiritual) preachers often engage in a heightened form of spoken language that is genuinely spontaneous, although they are drawing on oral formulas, memorized expressions, and standard phraseology that permeate the culture and can be inserted anywhere in the sermon. Folk preachers generally frown on the written sermon. No less a figure than the nineteenth-century revivalist Charles Grandison Finney defended the extemporaneous preaching of those who, like the folk preacher, did not believe in writing out their sermons. According to Finney,

Writing sermons had its origin in times of political difficulty. The practice was unknown in the Apostles' days. No doubt written sermons have done a great deal of good, but they can never give to the gospel its great power. Perhaps many ministers have been so long trained in the use of notes, that they had better not throw them away. Perhaps they would make bad work without them. . . . But it is objected to extemporaneous preaching, that if ministers do not *write*, they will not *think*. . . . Writing is not thinking. . . . The mechanical labor of writing is really a hindrance to close and rapid thought.[15]

Even today many young black seminarians who grew up listening to folk preaching in the extemporaneous style say they simply cannot write out their sermons beforehand. At best they can only start with a skeletal game plan in their minds that they fill out in an in-the-moment fashion once the oral performance is underway in the pulpit.

On the other hand, the intellectual preacher who is also in pursuit of artful language is engaged in oration as artificial rhetoric where language is filtered through the technology of writing.[16] Folk preachers hue much closer to conversational speech, using short phrases reminiscent of spoken rather than written language. And even when they do write out a sermon beforehand, they more often than not spontaneously translate it into sermonese in the pulpit.[17] The intellectual preacher writes out a sermon of carefully crafted speech and then declaims it from memory in the pulpit—Gardner Taylor, Manuel

Scott, E. K. Bailey, and A. Louis Patterson are prime examples of twentieth-century preachers who perfected this craft. Gardner Taylor, for example, wrote his sermons out by hand each week, carefully crafting each word, and then turned them over to his secretary no later than Friday. He would then spend time with the typed sermon on Saturday, reviewing it once more on Sunday morning in his office just before the beginning of the worship service. So particular was Taylor about his words that sometimes during the service he would step into the preacher room just off from the pulpit area and jot out notes by hand in order to get as close as possible to the crafted speech he had labored over the week before. In this sense Taylor was truly an intellectual preacher. Seldom, if ever, in public speaking did Taylor resort to any form of unadorned speech.[18] There are also intellectual manuscript preachers on the order of Charles Adams, Carolyn Ann Knight, William A. Jones, Sandy Ray, and Miles Jones, who read their crafted speech with great passion and precise diction.[19] The late C. L. Franklin and Caesar A. W. Clark were that rare amalgam of intellectual preachers who wrote their sermons out but preached them most heartily in the whooping style of the old-time folk preacher.[20]

Many intellectual preachers, with their written prose, tend to veer between the folk and intellectual style in the actual preaching of the sermon. Sometimes, especially for those who preach without notes, it is due to an inability to remember the exact phrasing of the crafted speech, and at other times it is a rhetorical device intended to demonstrate to the listening congregation that the preacher is not some highfalutin speaker far removed from the life situations of the gathered church. On such occasions the preacher purposely takes the written English of the sermon and translates it into conversational speech that is closer to "talking" as opposed to "speaking." Still other preachers unintentionally lapse into the less-formal speaking style even though they have spent much time on their stylized presentation. If they move wholly into the highly emotive spontaneous speech in the pulpit, later when they reflect on their sermon or hear a tape of their presentation, many preachers can be heard to complain that they sounded too black, which is to say, they veered too far from their prepared oratory off into the unadorned speech of casual conversation.[21]

Spontaneity is central to the folk preacher's style, and the appearance of spontaneity is central to the intellectual preachers even though they have crafted their oration down to the word in pen and ink. In the pulpit, the folk preacher and the intellectual preacher want to lay claim to divine inspiration in their preaching, for it is that claim that gives them their authority in the pulpit. Their authority comes when the congregation believes preachers are channeling God or that God is speaking through them.[22]

Historical Expressions of Crafted Oratory

Black preachers traffic in the currency of words. Historically they have taken great delight in crafting their formal stylized speech for the preached word. In his early years as dean of Rankin Memorial Chapel at Howard University, Benjamin E. Mays, later president of Morehouse College and mentor to Martin Luther King Jr., invited Vernon Johns, King's predecessor at Dexter Avenue Baptist Church, to deliver a lecture/sermon in part because Johns was such a great orator. Johns recounted the invitation in a sermon he delivered years later at Howard University:

> Dr. Mays wrote me that they were having a religious convoca-tion: the president of Catholic University was speaking for the Catholics; the president of the Jewish Theological Seminary was speaking for the Jews; a professor of the University of Paris was speaking for the Eastern Orthodox Church; and he said they wanted a colored man who was as good or better than any of them to speak for the Protestants. . . . Back in those days, I did not have a family and I still had my conceit, so when I read that, I was neither surprised nor offended when the letter said that I was the person.[23]

A review of a representative sampling of black preaching over the last three hundred years will demonstrate the power and ongoing appreciation for well-crafted rhetoric in the black church.

Absalom Jones (1746–1818)

In a sermon preached in thanksgiving for the end of the slave trade in 1801, Absalom Jones, cofounder with Richard Allen of the Free

African Society and founder of St. Thomas African Episcopal Church, Philadelphia, writes in the high language of well-crafted oratory:

> The history of the world shows us that the deliverance of the children of Israel from their bondage is not the only instance in which it has pleased God to appear in behalf of oppressed and distressed nations, as the deliverer of the innocent, and of those who call upon his name. . . . Yes, my brethren, the nations from which most of us have descended, and the country in which some of us were born, have been visited by the tender mercy of the Common Father of the human race. He has seen the affliction of our countrymen, with an eye of pity. . . . Dear land of our ancestors! Thou shalt no more be stained with the blood of thy children, shed by British and American hands, the ocean shall no more afford a refuge to their bodies, from impending slavery.[24]

Jones wraps the faithful God in language of a sympathizer who cares deeply for his children. From the language alone, one gets a sense of God as a loving, caring individual who has delivered his children from great turmoil and despair.

J. W. C. Pennington (1809–1871)

In the following extract we see an example of J. W. C. Pennington's emphatic style in a sermon delivered on the question of slavery in the Bible:

> Is the word of God silent on this subject? I, for one, desire to know. My repentance, my faith, my hope, my love, and my perseverance all, all, I conceal it not, I repeat it, all turn upon this point. If I am deceived here—if the word of God does sanction slavery, I want another book, another repentance, another faith, and another hope.[25]

Pennington in rapid-fire succession enumerates some of the bedrock words of the Christian faith—repentance, faith, hope, love—and promises to do away with all of them if the Word of God sanctions slavery. This crafted rhetoric may seem to some to be over the top, but Pennington uses language to make his case for just how repulsive he finds slavery to be.

Alexander Crummell (1819–1898)

In a Thanksgiving sermon given in 1877 Alexander Crummell uses the opportunity to say why Afro-Americans need to be grateful to God now and in the future. His lofty language leaves a despised people filled with an undiminished eschatological hope:

> Nothing, believe me, on earth; nothing brought from perdition, can keep back this destined advance of the Negro race. No conspiracies of men nor of devils! The slave trade could not crush them out. Slavery, dread, direful, and malignant, could only stay it for a time. But now it is coming, coming, I grant, through dark and trying events, but surely coming. The Negro—black curly-headed, despised, repulsed, sneered at—is, nevertheless, a vital being, and irrepressible. . . . With all these providential indications in our favor, let us bless God and take courage. Casting aside everything trifling and frivolous, let us lay hold of every element of power, in the brain; in literature, art, and science; in industrial pursuit; in the soil; in cooperative association; in mechanical ingenuity; and above all, in the religion of our God.[26]

Crummell uses language to describe that which is most despised in the Afro-American—black curly-headed, despised, repulsed, sneered at—to call attention to the great reversal that will one day take place in the lives of the people of African descent.

L. K. Williams (1871–1940)

L. K. Williams illustrates the eloquence of black spoken language in his sermon series on the book of Psalms, which he delivered to the Olivet Baptist Church in Chicago, Illinois. Note how he builds on the language of the Twenty-third Psalm to provide comfort and succor to the many in his congregation who had known hardship and tribulation:

> "The Lord Is," not has been, not going to be, but the Lord right now is my Shepherd. . . . Of it, Beecher said, "David left no sweeter. . . . It is the nightingale of the Psalms. It has filled the air of the whole world with melodious joy, greater than the heart can conceive. It has charmed more griefs to rest than all the philosophy of

the world. It has remanded to their dungeon more felon thoughts, more black doubts, more thieving sorrows, than there are sands on the seashore. It has sung courage to the army of the disappointed. It has poured balm and consolation in the heart of the sick, of captives in dungeons, of widows in their pinching grief, of orphans in their loneliness. Dying soldiers have died easier as it was read to them. It has made the dying slave freer than his master."[27]

Williams describes in picturesque detail what it means to have the Lord as one's shepherd. He personifies thoughts, doubts, and sorrows and sends them off to prison where they can no more harm those who trust in the providential hand of God.

Vernon Johns (1892–1965)

In a sermon delivered at Howard University's Rankin Memorial Chapel, May 16, 1965, titled "The Romance of Death,"[28] Vernon Johns makes use of both metaphor and simile as he speaks poetically about death's inevitability and finality:

The next thing about death after its certainty is as someone has said: "Strange is it not of the millions who before us passed the door of darkness, not one returns to tell us of the way?" We must travel, too. Death is not only certain, but death is a disaster which is complete and final. Unlike a wrecked car or a sinking ship, nothing can be salvaged from it. All sense and sensibility is destroyed. The waning subject is left blind and deaf and mute. Every joy and good of life is destroyed, becomes odorless and tasteless. The hand which desperately clutched the other in the twilight of vanishing sensation falls listlessly away and is felt no more, forever. The beauty which was once ardently courted turns not to ashes, as we eucharistically say—but to the most offensive corruption which by legal enactment must be buried beyond its power to contaminate those who are still alive.[29]

Johns uses the language of doom to describe the finality of death. Even for those who believe in the resurrection, Johns wants us first to understand the grimness and utter degradation of death. Before we can move on to see that which is redemptive about death, Johns wants to be certain that we have understood the utter hopelessness of that state of being.

Gardner C. Taylor (1918–)

The following is from President Gardner Taylor's message to the Progressive National Baptist Convention, Inc., in September 1968. Taylor uses language to contrast black hope and despair in a world where the absurd can at times appear normal:

> There is a power growing out of our experience of blackness in this land. There is much that is wrong, distorted, disfigured, crippled about us, but there are gifts and powers in the very limp which is our history here. There is a quality of rapture among black people which is authentically Christian. There is a sense of optimism which sees the threatening clouds of life but sees them shot through with the light of God. There is the gift and power of black people as members of the "disestablishment" to see the society in its splendor and shame. There is the power of a rhythmic beat orchestrated by trouble and mourning and hope which one hears in the strange, sad music of the black preacher when he moves honestly within the cultic setting.[30]

Throughout all the complexities and contradictions of black existence in America, Taylor sees optimism, even in the threatening clouds of life that are shot through with the light of God. He paints a picture of hope in the midst of hopelessness and optimism in the face of the threatening clouds of life.

Charles Adams (1931–)

The following comes from Adams's sermon titled "One Thankful Soul." With the skillful use of language, Adams will identify the Samaritan with the struggles of the marginalized throughout the world:

> But then all of a sudden, one of them, the odd ball out, the Samaritan, the one that was least loved because his future was still dim, even though he was healed of his leprosy, he was still hated because he was a Samaritan, in the wrong church, had the wrong ideology, had the wrong theology, was the wrong color. His skin was clear but it was darker. And he had every reason to feel bitter because he still had to face a mean and rejecting world. But this one who was disliked and discouraged and displaced and disrecognized

and dismissed and disregarded and disabled and disconnected and disrespected, just "dissed" one of them, when he saw that he was healed, turned around to find the source of his blessing.[31]

Using a barrage of words that begin with "dis," Adams points out that the marginalized Samaritan still found much for which to be grateful. The abundance of difficulties described by Adams is intended to convey to the listening congregation that they, too, in spite of all their difficulties can also find much for which to be grateful.

Prathia L. Hall (1940–2002)

Prathia Hall uses the story of the woman with an issue of blood to argue against the prejudices of a male-dominated hierarchy. It soon becomes evident that she is not simply speaking for the woman in the Scripture but speaking to oppressed women wherever they may exist:

Sisters and brothers, the story does not end here. The conclusion of this story is not what she told Jesus, but what Jesus told her. Throughout these two thousands years we have been told what women can and cannot do based on what this or that person said. Rarely have those who set the rules consulted Jesus. When they have even bothered to glance in his direction, they argue that there can be no women pastors and priests because there were no women among the twelve disciples. Yet this argument is absurd; there were no Gentiles among the twelve either. By that reasoning, we would disqualify just about every male in the public today. The real problem of these gatekeepers is that they have not watched Jesus closely enough. Let us not leave our sisters and her story without closely watching Jesus. It was the very nature of Jesus to engage in profoundly consequential reversals. He turned stuff around. If it was upside down, he set it right side up. The very purpose of his sojourn on earth was to reverse the death process—to give us eternal life, if we would but believe in him.[32]

Hall argues that just as Jesus engaged in profoundly consequential reversals so must those in contemporary times who are trying to bring about justice for oppressed women. She skillfully clothes her argument in incarnation language.

Language as Public Treasure

As the previous and brief three-century span of representative samples of black preaching clearly demonstrates, blacks do not attempt to get away from the rhetorical styles of an earlier generation. They lift them up and continue them. Crafted speech still has a powerful ring in the black church, and it still speaks to the hearts and minds of the black listening congregation. Henry Mitchell has rightly noted that the black worshiping congregation has enthusiastically embraced the well-turned phrase. In an earlier work I listed creative language as one of the long-standing defining characteristics of African American preaching.[33]

In short, the black church views language as a public treasure, unlike mainline traditions where language is regarded as a private domain, thus making attribution an essential component of white preaching. In black circles it is there for the enjoyment, benefit, and uplift of all. When black preachers hear something once and like it, most feel free to use it in their own preaching at some point. On first use they might say where they read or heard it, but from that time on many feel free to use it as their own. It is the language and not its source that's important. The black preacher has long known what the Scriptures clearly impart: "There is nothing new under the sun" (Eccl. 1:9). The traditional black church expects and appreciates rhetorical flair and highly poetic language in the preaching of the gospel. Blacks are taught early on to love words—to love how they sound, how they feel, how they create reality, and how they give voice to the deepest expressions of one's inner being.

Whites often do not see language this way. It was no less a figure than Reinhold Niebuhr who spoke of his opposition to pretty preaching—those ostentatious, ornamental flourishes—and his preference for the rough-hewn and plain-spoken sermons that the Reformed tradition has so much admired.[34] John Calvin, according to Reformed theologian John Leith, was the enemy of the ostentatious, the pompous, the contrived, and the needlessly complicated. Calvin saw language in a plain and unpolished manner as the servant of the truth.[35] Such cautions notwithstanding, there is little fear in black pulpits of being accused of "pretty preaching." In fact, seasoned pastors from an earlier generation could often be heard admonishing younger ministers not to be afraid "to preach a little." By that they meant, Don't be afraid to allow the Spirit of God through the power of language to lift the sermon to higher heights where transformation happens.[36]

Language as public treasure opens the black preacher to endless resources and limitless imaginative possibilities in the preparation of the sermon. Taylor Branch in *Parting the Waters* recounts the story of Martin Luther King Jr. sending his aide, Chauncey Eskridge, on a mission to find the eccentric Vernon Johns, King's predecessor at the Dexter Avenue Baptist Church in Montgomery, Alabama. King told Eskridge that he was hungry for some of John's ideas. King wanted all of the notebooks containing Johns's Sunday sermons. Eskridge found Johns in southern Virginia tending a squatter's vegetable stand:

> It took some time for Johns to adjust to the gravity of the request. When he did, he began ticking off sermon titles, then reciting snatches of sermons, and finally he began preaching in full animation on the dangers of drinking Pharaoh's wine. Eskridge stood there in the mud for the better part of an hour. Later he recovered enough of his legal skepticism to suspect correctly that the notebooks Johns promised to send did not exist—always his sermons returned to the air from whence they had come. King did not accept the lonely reality of such a conclusion. He insisted that there must be notebooks. Even after Johns died months later, he asked Eskridge whether any had arrived in the mail.[37]

King, regarded as one of the most able orators of the twentieth century, turned to a preacher from an earlier generation for ideas and rhetoric—sermons and speeches—to provide him with powerful rhetorical fodder for the struggle in which King was involved. Keith Miller in *Voice of Deliverance* shows time and time again where King borrowed from preachers on the order of Fosdick, Hammond, and many others.[38] This is not unusual in black preaching; it is par for the course.

Language as public treasure also relieves black preachers of having to create ex nihilo (out of nothing) each week. Instead they rely heavily on oral formulas and set pieces that can be inserted at many different places in the sermon. Black language itself is permeated with colorful speech, and there are pat phrases, clichés, and colloquial expressions that are understood immediately by the black masses. While many could be characterized as common platitudes, others are more oblique to those who have not grown up in the tradition. The black preacher is heavily dependent on these oral formulas.[39]

So why this continued love of language among black preachers? Blacks have historically loved language for a variety of reasons. First, *blacks believe that language empowers the marginalized.* Walter Ong has noted that oral speech is active, alive, and dynamic.[40] Rooted in the strong oral traditions of African culture, the act of public speech making, which calls for a more formal kind of speaking, has historically been much more than just a means of communication for the African American people:

> For early American blacks, bound in service to a land that claimed to be freedom-loving, public speaking was more than an important social instrument: it was a practical weapon against the power of slavery that sought to be all-controlling, a means to psychological and emotional survival, and a vehicle for maintaining personal dignity and self-respect. It was a means of resisting slavery's intent to reduce its victims to the level of subhuman property taking value solely from a master's appraisal.[41]

Second, *blacks use language to render God present.* Blacks are not shy about implementing such literary devices as antiphonality, repetition, alliteration, syncopation, oral formulas, thematic imagery, and so forth to get the Word across. They unabashedly use these devices to evoke a sense of God's awe and mystery in the listening congregation.

Unlike many European and mainline American denominations where architecture and classical music inspire a sense of the holy, blacks seek to accomplish this act through the display of well-crafted rhetoric. Hortense Spillers, in her work on Martin Luther King Jr. and the style of the black sermon, notes that historically blacks did not have the money for the Gothic cathedrals nor did they have the formal musical training required to master Bach and Beethoven on the organ, but they did have words.[42] Words are used in black preaching to create awe and mystery and to render present a God of power and might.

Black preachers have typically used language freely to describe who God is and what God is like. Crafted language that speaks of God's eternal vigilance, presence, and power is common in black pulpits:

> Long after centuries of civilization shall lie closed and completed, God shall reign supreme. Long after empires and nations lay buried in the graveyards of history, God shall reign supreme. Long after time runs out exhausted and collapses at the feet of eternity, God shall reign supreme. There is not when he was not, and there cannot be when he shall not be. He's back behind yesterday and he's up in front of tomorrow. Waves from two eternities dash upon his throne and yet he remains the same. He's older than time and senior to eternity. He was before was was. Back before the purple hills of eternity, before there was a who or a where a when or there, God was.[43]

Such constructs are common and are likely to be heard in any number of variations by black preachers from very diverse backgrounds. When language is regarded as a public treasure, black preachers feel no need to create out of nothing; instead they take the creative rhetoric that is already out there and make it their own.

Third, *blacks use language to call forth a world that does not exist*. Language is used to create an alternative world based on the promises of God. The language is often majestic because so much weighs on the outcome, and it is often poetic because one must suspend present-day realities even to fathom what is being spoken of. A primary example of this calling forth of an alternative world can be found in Martin Luther King Jr.'s "I Have a Dream" speech. Although the speech was delivered on a number of occasions by King in civil rights demonstrations in different parts of the country,[44] it was first heard by a large segment of the white population on August 28, 1963, during the March on Washington.[45] Speaking in his clearest diction and stateliest baritone, King used crafted speech—precise, polished, and reflective—to call forth a world that did not exist.[46] In fact, in the 1960s when King revealed the contents of his oration, it was so far from reality that he referred to it as a dream. He used language to create reality:

> I have a dream that one day this nation will rise up and live out the true meaning of its creed: "We hold these truths to be self-evident: that all men are created equal."

I have a dream that my four children will one day live in a nation where they will not be judged by the color of their skin but by the content of their character. . . .

I have a dream that one day the state of Alabama . . . will be transformed into a situation where little black boys and black girls will be able to join hands with little white boys and little white girls and walk together as sisters and brothers.

With language King spoke a world into existence that few believed in 1963 would ever come about. Some of those words would be picked up forty-five years later by the first African American to become president of the United States.

Fourth, *blacks use language to create an environment for belief.* Whites are more inclined to use language for information whereas blacks are more inclined to use it for inspiration. (Inspiration is one step removed from celebration.) Words, images, stories, slices of life, and so forth are rhetorical tools intended to create an environment where the listening congregation becomes comfortable trying the gospel on for size. In the best of black preaching, few words are wasted. All that is spoken is in service to belief. Every word, every argument, every proposition, every example, every slice of life, every quotation, every gesture, every instant of eye contact, and every pause are in service to belief. The preacher through the gift of language is attempting to create a context, a situation, an environment, if you will, for belief. Through the proclamation of the gospel, listeners are encouraged to enter into the biblical world (an alternative world) to see their plight and predicament; their hope and their future in Christ. Language is in service to belief.

Can this love of artful language survive the postmodern era, with its emphasis on diversity, otherness, and difference? Gardner Taylor and Robert Franklin are among those who have expressed concern that the traditional love of language in this style of preaching could well be lost to future generations of black preachers. Franklin has decried recent trends in some word-churches to move more toward the teaching sermon, that is, a more lecture-like teaching of biblical truths that focuses on building the personal faith of the believer while deemphasizing the black churches' traditional understandings of justice issues and its ability to use poetic language to express deep truths.[47] Franklin rightly notes that preaching is not philosophical argumentation but rather an invitation to take an imaginative journey. Preaching as imaginative journey engages the imagination and moves deeply into the human psyche. In so doing, says Franklin, it can lead to new ways of seeing the world, to decisions to change directions in life, and to new encounters with the holy. The flat language of the lecture is simply not able to give birth to this kind of spiritual transformation.[48] James H. Harris, who views the carefully wrought oral expressions of the African American preacher as a language that has historically extolled freedom and justice along with repentance and salvation, also expresses concern over the future shape of the black language world.[49]

This love of language may not last even though one can hear it in the preaching of Alexander Crummell, Francis J. Grimke, L. K. Williams, M. L. King, Charles Adams, Jesse Jackson, E. K. Bailey, and others. But there are hopeful signs on the horizon. A new generation of preachers is also employing this elaborately stylized speech in their preaching. Otis Moss III of the Trinity United Church of Christ in Chicago; Raphael Warnock, pastor of the historic Ebenezer Baptist Church in Atlanta, Georgia; and Raquel St. Clair, who holds a PhD in New Testament from Princeton Theological Seminary, are prime examples. All have been formally trained and must of necessity be categorized as "intellectual" preachers, but their rhetoric is reflective of the long-standing tradition of artful oratory in the black church.[50]

Chapter 8

On the Preparation and Delivery of Sermons

Settling into a Preparatory Rhythm

Sermon preparation is a subjective exercise that varies from individual to individual. While there are some basic procedures involved in the process, each preacher must employ those procedures in a manner best suited to his or her creative energies. All preachers have a "preparatory rhythm" in their innermost being that they must discover, get comfortable with, and settle into when attempting to prepare sermons on a weekly basis. Different preachers think themselves into creativity in different ways. A preacher's preparatory rhythm does not merely concern itself with the how-tos of sermon preparation but also with the mode of reflection best suited to reach the depths of the preacher's creative energies. Some preachers are most creative when they follow a step-by-step sermon preparation process. Their minds work best around a structured, well-defined to-do list. There are a number of helpful how-to manuals for this kind of structured preparation.[1]

Other preachers would find this very regimented approach to sermon creation stifling and overly burdensome. Consequently, they might begin their sermon preparation by meditating on a scriptural passage without the aid of scholarly tools or the expectation of a mandatory "next step." Some refer to this kind of meditative reflection as brooding or a silent sitting before God. Thinking through the fruitful possibilities in the text without any influence from outside sources or expectations of a formal process allows the scaffolding of a sermon to begin to take shape in their minds. The rhythm best suited for such preachers is meditative, not structured step-by-step instruction.

Others prefer to begin by focusing on the life situations (*sitz im leben*) of different individuals in their congregation, community, and/or larger world. These preachers believe that a steady gaze on lived experience will eventually lead them to what is universal in the whole of human experience.[2] They ease themselves into creativity by thinking about the people, not the biblical text—at least not initially. They are quite comfortable moving from lived experience to Scripture and back to lived experience. Sometimes their sermon preparation begins with a specific biblical text, and sometimes it does not. Even when they begin with a text, it is not the explication of the passage that is foremost in their minds. From start to finish they focus on the human situation with an eye toward understanding how the good news of the gospel makes its claim on that experience. In this approach some form of congregational exegesis rather than biblical exegesis takes the lead.[3] While scriptural explication will play an important role before the preacher's study time has ended, initially it must yield to the preacher's quest to reflect on where God is at work in human experience.

Still others begin the sermon preparation process by immediately consulting the published works of scholars. Barbara Brown Taylor begins her sermon preparation in a manner similar to this. Says Taylor, "I read a few commentaries to get me going, thinking first about the text, then about the world God loves, and finally about the particular congregation."[4] To converse with the scholars at the outset of the preparation process helps some preachers to get a genuine feel early on for the text, based on the informed reflections of sound biblical scholarship. Their rhythm is immediate engagement. Time spent imagining what might or might not be in the text at the outset of their study is not considered by them to be the best use of their time. Fred Craddock says his imagination takes flight when he knows what's actually going on in the text.[5] Thus some preachers' rhythms are best suited to immediate engagement with the informed insight of the scholars.

This immediate move to the commentaries should not be viewed as a shortcut but rather as an experienced cut usually taken by those with some years of preaching experience who are able to establish in short order the basic essentials of what the text is about. Preachers would do well to remember, however, that their conversation with the scholars should always be a two-way conversation. The scholars speak in general about the word while preachers search for a particular word to their congregation. The preacher will soon find out that often the scholars do not agree on what is going on in a particular passage of Scripture. In such instances the preacher should not hesitate to make a call based on the best information and insight available to him or her at that time. Editorial judgments will always have to be made on the part of the preacher in order to move the sermon preparation forward.

Some preachers are long-distance runners who prefer a deliberate, week-long buildup in the creation of a sermon. Many begin to think about next week's sermon soon after the Sunday preaching has been completed. As mentioned earlier, these preachers prefer a very methodical approach to sermon creation, some going so far as to assign certain tasks to certain days of the week.[6] However, there are also some very able preachers who prefer the rhythm of a sprint runner. They seem to work best under the hurried pressure of a Saturday night beginning and a fast-approaching Sunday morning deadline. They need to hear the ever-increasing roar of Sunday morning's train in order to get their creative juices flowing. From time to time all preachers have felt the anxiety of not having a completed sermon on Saturday night. But sprint preachers prepare their sermons in this hurried manner on a consistent basis. H. Beecher Hicks, pastor of the Metropolitan Baptist Church in Washington, DC, prefers this sprint-preparatory-rhythm style. Hicks says, "There is no way to avoid it. I confess. I am one of those proverbial Saturday-night preachers."[7] According to Hicks, on any given Saturday night he can be found with a Bible in one hand, concordance in the other, a computer ready to go, with a thesaurus propped up on the side.[8] Anyone who has heard Hicks preach would have to agree that this method seems to work quite well for him. Hicks, however, declares it to be an unhappy practice that is physically demanding, emotionally frustrating, and rarely producing power either in the sermon or in the preacher.[9] Yet he seems unable to break himself from this habit. His warnings notwithstanding, the Saturday night special appears to be a preparatory rhythm that works for many preachers; even those who are not bold enough to confess it like Hicks.

Getting a Sense of the Text

While the ways that preachers work themselves into their preparatory rhythms may differ, at some point scriptural exposition must enter the picture. Preachers must find an exegetical method that works and then hone it to such perfection that it becomes second nature to them. When it comes to the actual selection of a text, many preachers begin by reviewing the lectionary passages for the upcoming Sunday. Others are inclined to do series preaching that carries them through a continuous stretch of Scripture, thus relieving them of the responsibility of selecting a text each week. Some, while not hewing strictly to the lectionary, allow their selection of texts to be informed by the church calendar. Still others engage in what is known as preacher's choice, which means the preacher is responsible for selecting the text each week. Having grown up in the National Baptist tradition, I was shaped by preacher's choice, but I never considered it to be merely my choice. I always believed that I was allowing the Spirit to guide and direct me each week in my selection of a scriptural text. While there is much to be said for the lectionary preaching and its ability to cover large swaths of the Bible—thus preventing favoritism and narrowness in scriptural selection—human choice is still involved in the lectionary process, even when that choice comes by way of group consensus.[10]

In the employment of preacher's choice, I make a conscious effort to avoid hobby-horse preaching, special pleadings, and the possible development of a canon within a canon by reviewing scriptural selections from time to time throughout the year to make sure that certain books of the Bible are not being overly favored to the exclusion of others. I'm also guided in my choice of Scripture by the church calendar and by the special occasions to which I am often invited to preach as an itinerant preacher. Occasionally I will review five or six years of sermons in an effort to insure that I have not neglected the whole counsel of God in my selection process.

After the selection of the scriptural passage my next task is to get a sense of the text, by which I mean a clear understanding of the passage of Scripture before me. There are many fine exegetical methods for sermon preparation.[11] They each have their strengths and weaknesses. Whether the method that one chooses is formal or informal, implicit or explicit, some basic steps should be followed.

For me, the most foundational step is to get a clear understanding of the text. Many black preachers employ some form of historical-critical methodology in their sermon preparation. I count myself among them. If nothing else, this method helps us to get a handle on the text. The setting, occasion, purpose, authorial intent, the first hearers, the intended audience, and so forth are essential to gaining a plain-sense understanding of the passage. What is the genre of the text? Is it a narrative, parable, epistle, or psalm? Who are the characters in the text? What role do they each seem to be playing? There are also questions of historical and theological importance that grow out of the text. At different times different emphases will come to the fore in preparation. On some weeks a certain biblical character will catch the preacher's attention. For example, Mark says that as Jesus was passing by the blind man, he stood still. Ask yourself, what did Jesus see that so caught his attention that it caused him to stand still; to stop dead in his tracks, as it were? There could well be some preaching in that sudden stop. On another week a theological concept that grows out of an intensive focus on one of the epistles will take the lead. For example, knowing what we know about the fractured, divisive environment in Corinth, what does the apostle Paul intend to convey when he addresses the Corinthians as "those who are sanctified in Christ Jesus, called to be saints . . ." (1 Cor. 1:2)? A sermon on the meaning of sanctification as expressed in the life of this troubled church would be worthy of further investigation. How then are we to live when we have been set apart for service by God?

Make it a habit to look for deeper understandings in the text. In Mark 8:22–26 ("Some people brought a blind man to [Jesus] and begged him to touch him. . . ."), Jesus put saliva on the man's eyes and laid his hands on him. He then asked, " 'Can you see anything?' And the man looked up and said, 'I can see people, but they look like trees walking.' " Jesus then laid his hands on the blind man's eyes a second time, and the man's sight was restored. Mark says, "And he saw everything clearly." On the surface one could possibly see in this text a failed first effort on the part of Jesus. The sermon could be titled "Up Close and Personal" and go something on the order of this: Even if Jesus is not successful the first time he is determined to make us whole at all costs. Nothing is too hard for the Savior when you are in blessing range." A deeper look at the text, however, will not view the first touch as failure on the part of Jesus, but rather failure on the part of the disciples to decipher the true meaning of what it means to follow Christ.

Morna D. Hooker argues that the gradual recovery of sight could be symbolic of the disciples' poor progress in grasping the significance of Jesus.[12] According to Hooker, the constant inability of the disciples in the chapters that follow this scene to understand Jesus' teaching about suffering suggests that Mark regards the disciples as semiblind until the resurrection; until then they are in the position of the half-cured man who could barely distinguish between people and trees.[13] The story of the blind man and the second touch is really symbolic of our inability to hear and understand Jesus' teaching. The significance of what is taking place right before us often remains hidden from those who are still deaf and blind to the truth.[14] The focus then is not on a failed effort on the part of Jesus to heal but on our ongoing failure truly to see.

After many years of preaching, I usually ask such questions and ponder possibilities in my head. I jot down notes of those things that capture my attention as being unusual, unique, or eye-catching in a different way. Getting a sense of the text also means looking for divine initiative. Where is God in the text? Sermons are about God, and the preacher is charged with making God's case on Sunday morning. If you are ever struggling to bring a sermon to life, look for divine initiative in the text. Search for God's presence and God's promises. Ask yourself what is instructive about the text for faith and formation in the Christian life. How might contemporary hearers benefit from this text as proclaimed Word of God?

Sermon preparation is more a simultaneous act than a consecutive sequencing, by which I mean several things are happening at the same time in sermon preparation as opposed to things happening in an orderly fashion one right after the other. Preachers must be multitaskers at their study table. Thus, running alongside of my formal investigation into the text are my own imaginative thoughts about the passage. I engage in a three-fold imaginative exercise that moves me closer to the significance of the passage for the people for whom the sermon is being prepared. Sermons come together better when the preacher keeps an eye out for the people to whom they will be preaching. The most difficult sermon to prepare is an anonymous sermon—a sermon that is devoid of the faces, hearts, and concerns of people caught up in the absurdities, complexities, and contradictions of life. When the faces of those people join us in our study, the sermon takes on an unmistakable intensity. Generic sermons intended for anybody, anytime, anywhere are more often than not lukewarm in tone and less than compelling in intent. In phase 1, which I call *initial* imagination (see chap. 6, "Imagination and the Exegetical Exercise"), I freely allow questions, comments, and fruitful possibilities to rise to the surface of my initial look at the text. At this stage I "play" with the text. No question is too farfetched; no thought is too base or mundane. No preaching possibility is rendered inappropriate, and no inkling of possibility is declared beyond the pale. Initial imaginative thoughts are lawless, free to roam and free to recreate. I allow my mind and the text to play with one another—by which I mean I give myself the freedom to think, do, and imagine my way into a text without the sanctions of an enforcing authority. Creativity happens when there is nothing at stake other than the free-flow of ideas between my imagination, the text, and the lived situations of those on whose behalf I have gone to the text. In this phase I am witness (observer) to the text in preparation for witnessing (testifying) on behalf of the text on Sunday.[15] This initial playfulness helps to move me from observer to preacher. When I am *playing* with the text, it does not matter to me what informed authority (biblical scholars and others) have to say about the passage. My imagination has been granted the freedom to roam freely and engage the text as I see fit. I throw caution to the wind and allow myself to think of and through the limitless possibilities surrounding the text. It is here that text, subtext, and context are almost indistinguishable from one another.

Initial thoughts are a crucial part of the black preacher's preparation process. Styled now in formal homiletic theory as brainstorming, free association, or imaginative construals, in earlier works they were dismissed as unadulterated eisegesis—a reading into the text as opposed to exegesis where one sought to draw out the true meaning of the passage. Thomas Long, sensing the importance of initial thoughts, gets at some understanding of them through the brainstorming step in his homiletic. Long refers to it as the step in exegesis where the preacher begins the interrogation of the text by asking of the text every potentially fruitful question that comes to mind.[16] In black preaching initial thoughts are not simply limited to a questioning of the text, but these early thoughts also involve imputing to and signifying about the text. Black preachers are not merely asking what is going on in the text, they are declaring early on what they see and hear in the text when their sanctified imagination is set free to ponder what they believe the Spirit is saying to their particular congregation. Long, however, comes closer than most to capturing the full creative significance of this early stage of the sermon-creating process.

Many seasoned black preachers engage in this exercise early on. Those who were known to do so were often regarded as uninformed, shallow, and unfaithful to the true meaning of the text. Yet black preachers understood better than most that those initial thoughts, questions, and ideas about the text—some of which would be asked by the congregation when hearing the text read in worship—could give them some of their more creative sermonic material. Later in the process, those initial thoughts would have to be reigned in through scholarly research and further investigation of the text, but some of what bubbled up out of this initial free flow of ideas could be used in the sermon and often times turned out to be some of the more inspiring and insightful parts of the sermon. Many black preachers know the benefits of allowing the imagination to prance at full gait early on in their study time.

At stage 2 of the imaginative process, which I call *informed imagination,* I begin reading what the scholars have to say about the passage. Their work is most helpful, for it is at this stage that I begin to get an in-depth scholarly assessment of the text. But even as I read the scholars, in the back of my mind I can still hear the faint giggle of my time at play. In sermon preparation, if a smile does not cross your lips while you are doing your research or if a joyful chuckle does not bubble up from within at some unexpected discovery, then you are probably taking yourself and your exegetical exercise much too seriously. I personally prefer to read as many commentaries, essays, and related articles as I can about the scriptural passage I'm studying that week. I read and reread. I mark the books and jot down thoughts that come to me while I'm reading. If nothing strikes me as unusual or worthy of further examination, I keep on reading. I am privileged to have access to one of the greatest theological libraries in the world—Princeton's Speer Library—and I do my best to take advantage of that by combing the shelves and databases for whatever I can find that helps me better to understand the passage of Scripture before me.

I cannot stress enough the importance of reading when preparing a sermon. I read a mixture of both critical and devotional works. Devotional commentaries are intended to aid preachers in the sermon-building process, giving them different ways to approach the passage being studied for preaching. Critical commentaries focus more on a careful and critical investigation into the biblical text with little or no regard for how the finds of the research might be used in a sermon. Sometimes I gain nothing more than a sentence or two from a particular commentary, and at other times I will hit pay dirt where what I have read gives flight to my thoughts and helps to shape the essence and content of the sermon. I do not engage in percentages as to how much or how little information I take from the commentaries, nor do I find myself completely buying the line of argument being presented. I take some of the material I have gleaned from the commentaries and other essays and monographs and incorporate them into my thoughts on the passage. I then rewrite those finds into the rhythm of my own speech pattern at a later stage in the sermon preparation process.

When using the works of others, one must deal with questions of attribution. When should one provide attribution when citing the works of others? Where there is an outstanding idea, argument, or quote, or a particularly unique way of saying something that I have garnered from my time of study, I cite the author's name in the sermon. Otherwise I do not. For example, when researching a sermon on 1 Kings 17 where Elijah stands before Ahab and predicts a drought, Elijah is instructed by God to go to Zeraphath, where he can receive sustenance from a widow woman in that city. Elijah finds the woman and asks her for water and bread only to be told by the widow that she has only enough for herself and her son. At that point Elijah says to her, "Do not be afraid." Walter Brueggemann says that whenever you read the words "do not be afraid" in Scripture they represent an injection of hope into an impossible situation.[17] Clearly such a stirring explanation of the phrase "do not be afraid" is worthy of attribution. In time the preacher will get a feel for when to quote an individual and when it is more fitting to incorporate the more common thoughts of others into their own word-crafting ability.

Reverend Joseph Lowry, in his benedictory prayer at President Barack Obama's first inaugural celebration, quoted a version of an oft-repeated quip in the black community: "If you're white you're right, if you're brown stick around, but if you're black get back." Lowry made no effort to provide attribution to this well-known saying even though many in the country heard it from his lips for the first time on the presidential inauguration day. I've heard all too many sermons lose their rhythmic flow because a preacher is obsessed with attribution, often breaking into the flow of his or her sermon—with names, actual quotes, and citations—turning it into a verbal essay instead of a direct encounter with the living God. Again, I will only use the name of an author in the sermon when there is an outstanding idea or a particularly insightful quote.

The third stage of my imaginative work is *enhanced imagination*. Ideas don't stop coming once the sermon is preached; in fact, sometimes they come while the sermon is being preached. Here it takes the wisdom and experience of a seasoned preacher to know how to skillfully employ fresh ideas that burst in on one's consciousness while the sermon is being preached. The employment of these fresh ideas in the hands of an inexperienced preacher can cause the sermon to lose its focus and/or trail off in a direction that the preacher had not intended. When in doubt, save the fresh insight for a later occasion or continue on with the sermon as planned. Sometimes fresh ideas come all the more when one has completed the sermon and has some quiet time to reflect on its strengths and weaknesses. How many preachers have said to themselves after preaching a sermon, I think it might have gone over better had I done this or that? Self-evaluation of one's sermon can be a good thing. This is true especially if preachers don't use this time to simply beat upon themselves. The imagination can actually play a positive role at this point, for the preacher gets to take another shot at the sermon, perhaps structuring it in a way that better says what the preacher was aiming for originally. Enhanced imagination allows the preacher to incorporate those thoughts into the sermon when that text or that particular theme is dealt with on some occasion in the future. The use of the imagination at this third level is tantamount to gathering up the left over "fragments" of the mystery of preaching so that nothing may be lost (John 6:12).

Following this very intentional exegetical work, where structured sermon preparation and my imagination are placed in juxtaposition to one another, my sermon preparation enters a different phase. I begin to think about how the sermon itself will take shape. Before I begin the actual drafting of the sermon, I ask four critical questions:

1. Are the Scriptures taking the lead in the shape and development of the sermon?

This question does not concern itself with how many times you quote the Bible in a sermon. Repeatedly saying the name Jesus over and over again does not make for an effective sermon. Asking whether or not the Scriptures are taking the lead in the shape and development of the sermon concerns itself with whether or not the sermon is based on some sense of faithfulness to the content of the text and the sense in which it is to be understood as the proclaimed Word to a particular people on a particular day.[18] In other words, did the preacher base his or her sermon on the thoughts, ideas, or insights growing out of the text? Has the text been allowed to speak anew or has the preacher approached the text with blinders on, determined that it will say what the preacher has always heard it saying or what the preacher has been brought up to believe that it is saying?

2. Is there a clearly defined controlling thought for this sermon?

The preacher needs to have a clear, defining thought in his or her mind about what the sermon aims to say. Aim is very important, for as the famed nineteenth-century preacher Henry Ward Beecher noted, "If you aim at nothing you will hit nothing!" While it may take some time to arrive at this desire for clarity, it should always be in the back of the preacher's mind. Far too many sermons end up being little more than pearls without a string—lots of scattered thoughts, good phrases, illustrations, and helpful hints that have no binding cord because they lack a clearly defined focus. Even though different people in the congregation will hear different things, when the sermon is finally preached, it is nonetheless the responsibility of the preacher to aim clearly and simply for a controlling thought that runs like a golden thread throughout the sermon. The controlling thought should be expressed in a simple declarative sentence of what the sermon is about, what the sermon aims to say. It is based on what the preacher perceives to be the claim of the text on those who will hear the sermon.

3. Is the sermon lucid and clear enough to be followed with the listening ear?

Sermons are not verbal essays but rather oral performances in real time that are meant to be heard. While many sermons will find their way to the printed page, they should be written with the clear understanding that at some point they will be spoken by the preacher and heard by the congregation. Charles Bartow has rightly noted that written texts are but an arrested performance.[19] They must be brought to life through the spoken word. The ear has priority in preaching, for before a sermon can be understood, it must first be heard. The sermon thus needs to be written in such a fashion that it can be easily followed with the listening ear. This is not to suggest that sermons should be "dumbed down" for public consumption; it is to suggest, however, that the crafted language of the sermon should be lucid, precise, and clear. Rewrites are a preacher's best friend. Sermons should employ an economy of words. There ought to be a clear purpose for every sentence in the sermon. Ostentatious fluff and imprecise language have no place in a tightly worded sermon written for the ear. When one reaches the writing stage, every word of the sermon should be spoken out loud before the preacher reaches the pulpit. In the writing and rewriting of the sermon, vocalizing it helps to bring clarity to thought and precision to writing. Long, drawn-out sentences are a no-no, for they constitute noise in the communication channel when people are trying to follow the argument of the sermon with their ears. Sermons written for the ear are conversational in tone and filled with sharp, crisp, descriptive language. Often in the black church someone in the congregation can be heard to say, "Paint the picture, preacher." This word of encouragement is intended to remind the preacher that people are listening and need him or her to provide mental pictures with language to help them see the gospel.

4. What does the sermon cause the listener to want to do?

Sermons ought to make the listener want to do something. The best sermons make some kind of claim on our lives. We do not preach for the listeners' enjoyment or entertainment, nor do we preach merely for the sake of argument. The preacher should have a specific goal in mind when thinking through the intended impact of the sermon on the listening congregation. Sermons can inform, encourage, inspire, teach, admonish, implore, edify, and so forth, but they urge us toward action. They call forth decisions about how we will or will not live out our lives in the presence of the Almighty. The preacher should have a clear sense of how the sermon will function. While listeners may carry something completely different away from the preaching moment, this in no way relieves the preacher of the responsibility to aim at a desired outcome. Even when we aim for specificity in our preaching, we must be ever mindful that the Spirit will have its way; sometimes reaching people through us and at other times reaching people in spite of us. The miracle of Pentecost where each person hears in his or her own tongue happens more often than we know.

Writing the Sermon

Sometimes I begin the initial writing of the sermon with a clear understanding of how the controlling thought will shape the sermon. At other times, even with my controlling thought in hand, I begin writing more on a hunch than on a clearly defined path. Often, in all honesty, how best to convey the controlling thought doesn't crystallize for me until I have begun the actual writing of the sermon. In one instance I'll begin with the explication of the passage; in another I will begin with some anecdote or slice of life before moving to the passage. I tinker with it until it feels right and sounds right to me. Some preachers, with their controlling thought in hand, can see clearly from beginning to ending how their sermon will be structured even before they have written one word. I have never been so fortunate. I begin in a very halting and tentative way by writing what I know and adding to it. I confess that I can get at it no other way. For me, an effective sermon will have no fewer than five or six major rewrites. It is, however, in the writing and rewriting that clarity begins to happen and that fruitful possibilities turn into focused arguments.

Most of the time I begin by writing a condensed version of what I believe to be the essence of the passage. This is one of the reasons exegesis is so important to me. If I don't have a good sense of the passage, I will not have a good feel for the sermon. I view the beginning stages of my writing almost as a lawyer's summation before the jury. In as clear and concise a manner as I can, I make every effort to lay before the listener my client's case. The tone and tenor of what is written is purposely subdued because I don't want to promise more than I can deliver. As I put my thoughts to writing, anticipating the moment when it is time for me to stand and deliver, I think of myself as a witness inviting people to come and see what I have heard and seen in the text. As I write, anticipating the preaching moment, I identify more with the woman at the well who urged her companions to come see a man who told her all that she had done rather than the carnival barker inviting people to an entertaining freak show.

Whether I begin writing on the biblical text or the human situation, I make every effort to be precise and clear; to be interesting, but not entertaining. Often the final product will look quite different from the initial writing. But writing helps me to focus. In a manner that is difficult to explain, at some point during the reading/writing process, I get a breakthrough where that wonderful collaboration between intuition, discipline, and creativity suddenly appears before me. That's when my mind and my imagination catch the rhythm of the sermon with my head and my typing skills race to keep pace. When these breakthroughs happen, I continue to write. I don't use breakthrough time to polish the language of the sermon. Polish only works when you have something to polish. Rather, I use these opportunities to gather fodder for the sermon. Writing under the intense heat of inspiration or, to mix metaphors, striking while the iron is hot demands that you get the ideas down on paper or computer screen as fast as you can. There will be plenty of time to clean up the language and verify the facts. Get it down on paper while it is coming. When you are researching and writing your sermon, if these breakthroughs don't happen you must pursue your reading/writing with the tenacity of an Elisha waiting on the elder Elijah to give him a double portion of his spirit. The imagination can be trained and implored to hold steady until inspiration comes. Like Jacob wrestling with the angel at the river Jabbok, don't let your writing go until your imagination blesses you. Wrestle with it all night if you must, but don't let it go. Too many preachers give up too quickly in sermon preparation, settling for a shoddy, superficial presentation of the gospel. Wrestle with the text. Pursue your line of inquiry. Keep reading, researching, and intuiting your way into the text until it yields its deep treasures. Inspiration will come. I recall quite vividly standing one afternoon in the study of that great Brooklyn preacher Gardner Taylor. I asked Taylor what he did in those instances when the sermon simply would not come together. He pointed to a window in his study facing toward the east and said to me, "I've seen the sun come up many a morning sitting at my study table." Taylor said those words with a certain sadness and longing in his voice. At the time of the interview he was already in retirement, and he appeared to think of his study time once more with a certain relish to return to the weekly challenge. I thought to myself, If more of us were willing to toil at our study tables until we, too, could see the sunrise, I'm convinced we'd have even better preaching today.[20]

Polishing the Language

Sermon creation is messy. It's akin to a construction site where many things are strewn about from the building project that has just taken place. When I have the rough form of the sermon in hand, I always spend some time cleaning up and polishing the language. Crafted speech continues to be a much-prized form of communication in the black church (see chap. 7 on artful language). When I argue for crafted speech, I'm not arguing for stilted ostentatious language but rather descriptive language that helps bring life and energy to the word that will be spoken into the hearing and the hearts of the people. Crafted speech also tightens the sermon up and prevents wasted words and unnecessary clutter in our speech when proclaiming the gospel. Another positive aspect of crafted speech is that it helps to create a rhythmic flow in the preacher's speech pattern, thus making the presentation more palatable to the listener. St. Augustine rightly argues that the sermon should teach, *delight*, and persuade.[21] Finally, crafted speech helps to enflesh the gospel. It doesn't simply make a point; it helps the congregation to envision in the mind's eye the concept that is being argued. Take for example Acts 17 where the apostle Paul is presenting the gospel of Jesus Christ to the Athenians and the foreigners who were living there. When trying to describe the type of city in which Paul was preaching, one could merely give a matter-of-fact description of a formerly great city that prided itself on learning and scholarship. Take for example the description of the city provided by F. J. Foakes Jackson and Kirsopp Lake in their commentary on Acts:

> If Paul approached Athens from the North, he would see the high hill of Lycabettos on his right, the Acropolis in front of him, and the Areopagus to his left. He would come in through the business section of the city, and walk up a shallow depression with an elevation on each side.[22]

Hans Conzelmann, who argues that the entire scene should be seen as a literary creation on Luke's part, is also devoid of energy and vitality in his description of the city:

> The might of Athens had been broken long ago, but the city still enjoyed great respect. . . . It should not be called a "quiet little city." It was a tourist center, site of great festivals, and still the classical university city.[23]

Jackson, Lake, and Conzelmann give us a bare-bones description of this historical city into which Paul has entered and is now preaching/ arguing. It is the preacher's responsibility, however, to make this city come to life when painting a description of it for the listening congregation.[24]

What follows is a description of Athens from a sermon titled "Why Bother?":

> Athens had seen and heard it all. In Paul's day, this once great and proud city was still considered the cultural and intellectual capital of the Roman Empire. It was a city steeped in art, literature, and learning. Of long-standing it had its names and its heroes and thus was not easily impressed by the new or the now. It was the place where Socrates, Aristotle, and Plato had lived and taught. And still counted among its sacred places was the Academy of Plato, the Lyceum of Aristotle, the porch of Zeno the Stoic and the garden of Epicurus. The voices of her poets had been heard throughout the civilized world and the hands of her artists had filled her streets and temples with images of the gods. It was said of Athens that while strolling her streets you were more likely to meet a god than

you were a man or a woman. Her myriad buildings and works of art stood in silent testimony to her former glory and grandeur. Even though Luke goes to great lengths to create for us this scene where Paul is standing face to face with the philosophers in their own town and on their own turf, the upstart Christian gospel still comes off as out of place. It just doesn't seem to fit in Athens. The gospel seems to be out of its league in a city like Athens. Athens is a tough place to speak the gospel.[25]

Crafted speech helps to bring the sermon to life. It dispenses with the fog of unnecessary verbiage, tightens up the language of the sermon, and greatly enhances the descriptive powers of the preacher. The preacher is after precision and clarity in the crafting of language. Crafted speech helps the listener not only to hear but also to see. Blacks have traditionally learned this kind of crafting through the oral tradition. Of long-standing there has been a deep appreciation in black churches for the manner in which language evokes a sense of the presence and power of God. Crafted speech repeated over and over again soon makes its way into what Bruce Rosenberg describes as an oral formula, that is, the skillful manipulation of metrically consistent phrases that enable the preacher to spin out narratives at great length.[26] But oral formulas do more than provide the preacher with a ready resource of quotes and usable materials; they also teach preachers how to catch the rhythm and creativity inherent in crafted speech; they teach preachers how to become wordsmiths in their own right.

Structuring the Sermon

After one has a sense of the text and pretty much gotten underway with the writing of the sermon, the sermon manuscript should then be set to movement in order to give it vitality and dynamism. There are at least two ways to outline a sermon manuscript: vertical and horizontal. The vertical outline (see Example A) tends more toward discursive, rationalistic thought. It lends itself to more of what the sermon is *saying* while the horizontal movement (see Example B) lends itself to what the sermon is *doing*. The difference between these two approaches can be seen in the structuring of a sermon titled "What

Are You Afraid Of?" based on the parable of the Talents found in Matthew 25 (see appendix B for the sermon):

> [14]"For it is as if a man, going on a journey, summoned his slaves and entrusted his property to them; [15]to one he gave five talents, to another two, to another one, to each according to his ability. Then he went away. [16]The one who had received the five talents went off at once and traded with them, and made five more talents. [17]In the same way, the one who had the two talents made two more talents. [18]But the one who had received the one talent went off and dug a hole in the ground and hid his master's money. [19]After a long time the master of those slaves came and settled accounts with them. [20]Then the one who had received the five talents came forward, bringing five more talents, saying, 'Master, you handed over to me five talents; see, I have made five more talents.' [21]His master said to him, 'Well done, good and trustworthy slave; you have been trustworthy in a few things, I will put you in charge of many things; enter into the joy of your master.' [22]And the one with the two talents also came forward, saying, 'Master, you handed over to me two talents; see, I have made two more talents.' [23]His master said to him, 'Well done, good and trustworthy slave; you have been trustworthy in a few things, I will put you in charge of many things; enter into the joy of your master.' [24]Then the one who had received the one talent also came forward, saying, 'Master, I knew that you were a harsh man, reaping where you did not sow, and gathering where you did not scatter seed; [25]so I was afraid, and I went and hid your talent in the ground. Here you have what is yours.' [26]But his master replied, 'You wicked and lazy slave! You knew, did you, that I reap where I did not sow, and gather where I did not scatter? [27]Then you ought to have invested my money with the bankers, and on my return I would have received what was my own with interest. [28]So take the talent from him, and give it to the one with the ten talents. [29]For to all those who have, more will be given, and they will have an abundance; but from those who have nothing, even what they have will be taken away. [30]As for this worthless slave, throw him into the outer darkness, where there will be weeping and gnashing of teeth.'"

For each method, first outline the sermon's controlling thought, its function, and its good-news message:

The controlling thought: Fear causes us to act irresponsibly with that which God has entrusted to us for a season.

The function of the sermon: To create a sense of urgency in the listeners to participate fully in life and use every gift God has so graciously bestowed upon us.

The good news: There is still time to use the gifts we have been given.

Example A

THE VERTICAL OUTLINE: What I will *say* in the sermon (deductive/propositional)

I. Explication of the text—Three people on the receiving end of money. Fear caused the person with one talent to act irresponsibly with that which had been entrusted to him for a season.

II. We are all afraid of something.
The past
The present
The future

III. That which we fear eventually manifests itself in our lives somehow.
A loss of direction
A loss of verve and vitality
An overwhelming sense of inadequacy

IV. Fear keeps us from using all that God has given to us in this life.
There is not a person living to whom God has not given something.
God never gives anything everything—the peacock.
We could come to peace if only we could realize that we are where we are supposed to be—the little boy in the field.

V. The text—the person with one talent focused too much on what he did not have.

VI. The Good News! There is still time for you to use the gifts that have been given.

Example B

THE HORIZONTAL OUTLINE: What I will *do* in the sermon
(The boxes indicate movement.)

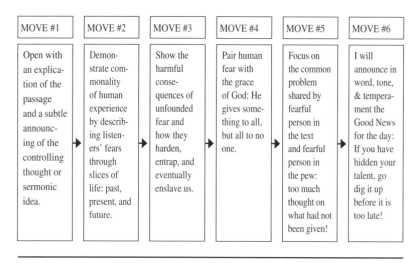

MOVE #1	MOVE #2	MOVE #3	MOVE #4	MOVE #5	MOVE #6
Open with an explication of the passage and a subtle announcing of the controlling thought or sermonic idea.	Demonstrate commonality of human experience by describing listeners' fears through slices of life: past, present, and future.	Show the harmful consequences of unfounded fear and how they harden, entrap, and eventually enslave us.	Pair human fear with the grace of God: He gives something to all, but all to no one.	Focus on the common problem shared by fearful person in the text and fearful person in the pew: too much thought on what had not been given!	I will announce in word, tone, & temperament the Good News for the day: If you have hidden your talent, go dig it up before it is too late!

While these two approaches may appear very similar on paper, in the actual performance of the sermon, distinguishing between what you will *say* and what you will *do* makes a huge difference in the movement and flow of the sermon. One approach tends to be pedantic and discursive while the other tends to be more lively and engaging. To structure a sermon around movement as opposed to argument keeps it from growing stale and static. There is a certain energy and vibrancy to the argument when the preacher is focused on movement in the text and in the sermon.

Preaching without Notes

To preach with or without notes—which way is best? There is no right or wrong answer. It depends on the personal preference and preaching style of each preacher. If one chooses to learn how to preach without notes, there are any number of viable ways. What is offered here is a method that works for me. It is not the only way to learn, nor is it necessarily the best way to learn. I am confident, however, that with a little time and serious commitment one can experience the powerful effect of learning to look at your congregation instead of your notes. Barry Black, the chaplain of the U.S. Senate, said you should take just enough paper in the pulpit to start a fire under your sermon.[27] To preach without notes does not mean you preach without preparation. I urge all those who preach without notes to write out a full manuscript, one that has been edited and reedited in order to make sure the language is precise, the moves are clearly defined, and the connecting links are in order. The memory work that's required to preach without notes comes at the end of the sermon preparation process. The preacher should never waste time trying to remember an unedited manuscript that may or may not make it to the pulpit. Memory work is reserved for the sermon as final product.

The first things I commit to memory are the broad moves of the sermon.

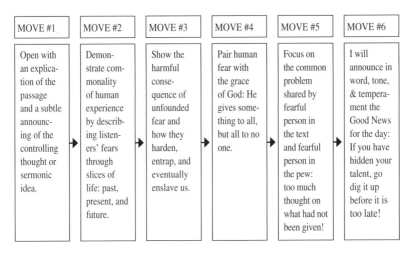

MOVE #1	MOVE #2	MOVE #3	MOVE #4	MOVE #5	MOVE #6
Open with an explication of the passage and a subtle announcing of the controlling thought or sermonic idea.	Demonstrate commonality of human experience by describing listeners' fears through slices of life: past, present, and future.	Show the harmful consequence of unfounded fear and how they harden, entrap, and eventually enslave us.	Pair human fear with the grace of God: He gives something to all, but all to no one.	Focus on the common problem shared by fearful person in the text and fearful person in the pew: too much thought on what had not been given!	I will announce in word, tone, & temperament the Good News for the day: If you have hidden your talent, go dig it up before it is too late!

A sermon will generally have four to six moves in it. Committing the broad moves to memory assures that I will always be conscious of where I am in the sermon and what I'm trying to argue at any point in the sermon. If memory fails me, I think about where I am in the move and then proceed to the next logical line of thought in the move. An awareness of where I am in any particular move helps to trigger my memory and keeps me pretty much on track in the delivery of the sermon. After memorizing the broad moves of the sermon, I then begin memorizing the paragraphs that make up the moves of the sermon.

MOVE #1

Open with an explication of the passage and a subtle announcing of the controlling thought or sermonic idea.

In the text before us this morning there are three people on the receiving end of money. Although the text says talent, we know that a talent in biblical times was a measure of money. One person was given five talents, another was given two, and a third was given one. According to some estimates, one talent was the equivalent of 15 years of a laborer's wages. So, you can see all three people in the text have been given a substantial sum of money for the purpose of trading with it profitably in their master's absence.

The person who had received five talents went immediately to put his master's money to work. The person who received two talents went immediately to put his master's money to work, but the one who received one talent, he dug a whole and buried his master's money in the heart of the earth. After a while the Lord of those slaves returned and called them to give an account of what they had done with that which had been given to them for a season. May I say here it doesn't matter what you have, what you know, or where you have been. What you have is only yours for a season. One day the Lord will return and call us to give an account of our stewardship.

The person who had received five talents was happy to make his report. When you have done your best, you don't mind making your report. He said, "Lord, you gave me five talents. See. I have increased them to ten." His master said, "Well done, good and faithful servant . . ." The one who received two talents stepped up to make his report. He said, "Master, you gave me two talents, I am happy to report that I have increased them to four." His Master said, "Well done, good and faithful servant . . ." Do you get the drift of the text? It does not matter how much they had been given. As long as they did the best they could, they received the same words of commendation from the Master: Well done, good and faithful servant.

When it came time for the one who had received one talent to report, he started scratching where he was not itching and grinning when nothing was funny, and instead of moving toward his master he began to do the back step. He said, "Master, I knew what kind of man you were and because of that I did nothing with what you gave me. Here it is just like you gave it to me with a little dirt on it." From his Master he received no word of well done; no word of good and faithful servant. Fear caused him to act irresponsibly with that which had been entrusted to him for a season.

I get comfortable with each paragraph in the move before going on to the next. When I have a feel for each paragraph in a move, I proceed to the next move and begin the process of memorizing all over again. I do this until all six moves along with their content-laden paragraphs have been committed to memory in a way in which I feel comfortable enough to head to the pulpit without the manuscript. The process is rather simple and takes only a couple of hours of preparation once one settles into the routine.

Preparation, writing, memorizing, and speaking all involve an internal rhythm that all preachers possess. Learning to synthesize those rhythmic patterns can be a great aid in helping the preacher to prepare, remember, and then deliver a sermon with conviction and authority. As is the case with most preachers, when it comes to sermon preparation, I have good days and bad days. There are times in my study when I am convinced, even after all these years, that God has called the wrong person to this task. The preparation process at times yields a sermon that I believe to be pulpit worthy, and other times it yields a sermon that causes me to make my way to the pulpit praying that I can make it through without doing too much damage to the Word of God and the people of God. Often I have discovered that the same guiding hand that upholds me also humbles me. In spite of all the ups and down of preparation, I still count it as one of the most rich and rewarding experiences in my life.

Chapter 9

How Does One Get Better
at the Foolishness of Preaching?

*S*isyphus, a character in Greek mythology, angered one of the great gods and was condemned to pushing a stone up a hill for eternity. Every time the stone reached the top, it would roll back down, forcing him to roll it up once again. At times the routinization and the cyclical task of preparing to preach can appear to subject the preacher to the pain and agony of Sisyphus. Often when thinking about all the work that's involved in preparation, preachers ask themselves, Is it worth all this effort? Does preaching really matter? Does the average parishioner expect his or her preacher to be a Martin Luther King Jr. or a Gardner Taylor? A Susan Johnson Cook or a Vashti McKenzie? Are there just people who are born to the craft? People whose preaching is better by nature than ours? And are we making too much of "effective" preaching? Isn't preaching just one of any number of things people look for in their minister?

As reported in *Time* magazine, the number one question people who serve on pulpit search committees want to know is, Can he or she preach?[1] A Methodist pastor in Dallas, Texas, once told the legendary black preacher Caesar Clark that he did not do a lot of yelling and shouting at his people. Instead, he told Clark, "I give my people what they need on Sunday morning." To which Clark said, "Well, if you don't give them a little of what they want on Sunday mornings, they won't be there for you to give them what they need." Many congregations are finding that maintaining vibrant education and outreach programs and a host of other ministries in their church and community depend on getting people to come to church in the first place. And getting people to come to church depends a lot on what they hear coming from the pulpit each Sunday.

Therefore, included among the many questions about preaching should be this one: "How does one get better at the foolishness of preaching?" In the first instance, I believe you get better at preaching by listening to preaching; by listening to preachers in whom you have found something you admire. Preaching is one of those oral/aural events where you can actually improve your own preaching by listening to the sermons of others. And I do mean "listen," for there is so much that is lost in written sermons, such as intonation, inflection, pace, emphasis, gesture, a twinkle in the preacher's eye, an unrehearsed moment of humor, and so forth. But there is much to be learned in listening. This is sometimes hard to believe, but I see men and women come to seminary who have never really heard the gospel. When they finally hear it, a light comes on for them. Almost to a person those who have shown some promise and some improvement in preaching are those who have exposed themselves or been exposed to good preaching. Those who grew up listening to a pastor who was faithful each Sunday to the preaching assignment or those who were privileged enough to attach themselves to some preacher who made a great impression on them actually fare better in the development of their preaching skills. Listening to the preaching of others is a great way to learn how to develop your own preaching skills.

I know there are people who say, "Oh, no, that's terrible. You shouldn't copy or imitate anyone else. You ought to be your own person in the pulpit." To that I say, "You are absolutely right." It was George Buttrick, the great American preacher of a generation past, who so ably reminded us that preachers are not parrots. Wise preachers, said Buttrick, will study the masters but they will not mimic them.[2] But I also say to you that you will have plenty of time to be your own person. But never deprive yourself of the opportunity to go and listen to someone whose preaching you admire, and then ask yourself, What in that sermon's content, form, style, and delivery made that a meaningful sermon to me? Why did I feel like I was in the presence of the Holy while that person was up speaking?

Why did I feel that I had been addressed by God while that person was preaching the gospel? Paul Scherer in *For We Have This Treasure,* admonished every preacher to be himself or herself, for God made you a unique individual with your own peculiar contribution to make.[3] But at the same time Scherer recognized that there were traits and characteristics in other preachers from which we could all benefit. You do not listen in order to mimic or imitate; you listen with an eye toward reflecting on those things in the preacher's sermon that enable you to set a standard of achievement by which to gauge your own preaching.

We all go through stages in our perceptions and evaluations of what constitutes good preaching. I remember now with fondness some of the Texas preachers I so admired when I was a boy. Their names live even now in my memory: Paschal Sampson Wilkinson Sr., Henry Clay Dilworth Jr., John Henry Mosley, and Abraham Lincoln Randon from Victoria. Even though they taught me much, I recognize that I, in a manner of speaking, have outgrown that preaching and am now at a different place and time in my own preaching journey. But listening to them gave me a leg up, and I hear their voices even now when I am trying to preach in the twenty-first century. I still hear the voices of those old preachers, for they taught me the fundamentals of preaching long before I reached the formal training of the seminary.

Second, one becomes a better preacher through study and persistence. Gardner Taylor, in his Lyman Beecher Lectures, said if you're having trouble getting a sermon together, often what is needed is to apply yourself more fervently to the seat of a chair.[4] Preachers, says Taylor, "want to recline, whine, and shine." But if you're going to shine on Sunday, you have to do something more than recline and whine through the week. Nothing is gained in preaching that does not come from diligent study. Again Paul Scherer reminds us that the first step toward a good sermon is hard work; the second step is more hard work; and the third is still more.[5] Fred Craddock says there is something to be had in going to the same place, to the same room, and sitting before that blank piece of paper (or computer screen) that gets the creative juices flowing more easily. "I know when I come to this room, to this place, to this computer it is time to think about preaching."[6]

That is my concern with the ease and access to sermons through the Internet. Good sermons, I believe, are born through diligent study and persistent struggle to bridge the distance between what the text meant and what it means. Good sermons are born of wrestling with the text and wrestling with the people of God who are on your heart at the hour of preparation. Karl Barth in "The Need and Promise of Christian Preaching," says, "They—the people of God—come Sunday in and Sunday out for they want to know if there is a word from the Lord and is it true?" And, says Barth, they want us to take them more seriously than they take themselves. They say to us in their continual coming, "Is it true? Is it true that there is in all things a meaning, a goal, and a God?"[7] That's what we have to struggle to get at in our preaching.

Go ahead, if you will, and get your sermons from the Internet, for there is nothing new under the sun. We all borrow from people. We have all heard and used a well-turned phrase, idea, concept, or point—hopefully with attribution. But to out-and-out use another person's sermon word-for-word will not in the end make you a better preacher. If you are consistently borrowing from others and taking shortcuts, how do you develop your own creativity? How do you develop the biblical expertise that comes from returning to a book of the Bible from time to time to preach on it—each time gaining a little more and storing away a little more for future reference? How do you come to some understanding of what works and why when you are trying to pair that sermonic idea or scriptural insight to the human situation? How do you learn to "pair" and "bridge" if you are always using someone else's blood, sweat, and tears?

Third, I think you become a better preacher through desire. In the best of preaching, scriptural text and heartfelt desire are united in a two-pronged search for what the text meant then and what it means now, with the Holy Spirit serving as the appropriate mediator. There is a sense in which the sermon preparation time is an act of worship. It is not simply some technical/skills-oriented exercise separate and apart from the transformation we seek to evoke in others through the power of the Holy Spirit. Before the sermon preparation process can begin in earnest, there must be in the preacher an unquenchable inner desire to proclaim the word. That has been one of the great strengths of the black church: it continues to imbue its young people with a desire to preach.

Fourth, you become a better preacher by living with the Scriptures. It is Father Walter Burghardt who reminds every preacher "to look ahead to next Sunday's sermon not as a chore but as a chance, not as an obligation but an opportunity." The faithful in front of you, says Burghardt, do not expect you to reduce the national budget or bring peace to [to the world]. They ask only that you speak to them of the God who has spoken to you—spoken to you through books and the Book, on your knees and on your streets, as you live and minister among the people.[8]

Sometimes the initial spark for a sermon comes from an event that seems totally unrelated to Scripture. It can be sparked by reading a novel or a newspaper, or by watching a movie or a Broadway play. Often the initial spark of Scripture meeting desire can be ignited when we hear others preach or hear a gifted professor bring an arcane or common passage of Scripture to life.

Everyday life experiences both common and catastrophic can also serve as the initial meeting points between Scripture and heartfelt desire. Sometimes it is life experience that leads us to fasten onto some scriptural text; at other times it is the text itself that causes us to ponder the human situation. Either way, in order for a sermon to begin to take shape there must be this initial coming together of desire and text. Wrestling with a text that speaks to you means selecting a text where desire and text meet and go forward together into further textual and situation-in-life investigation.

Fifth, one becomes a better preacher by continually focusing on the people who will be sitting before you. I asked Gardner Taylor, the dean of black preachers, if he ever had difficulty getting a sermon together. He confided in me that from time to time he experienced great difficulty in sermon preparation. "What do you do when that happens?" I asked. Taylor said he would go and visit the sick members of his congregation and remember once again the people who so desperately needed to hear the comforting word of God. From time to time we all need to think once again of the people who sit before us when we preach:

- A bereft soul for whom the heavens seem shut
- A single mother struggling to raise her children
- A person working on a miserable job for a miserable boss
- A spouse who has sacrificed his or her future for the other's career
- Anxious parents who've not heard from an absent child
- Some woman who feels trapped in a situation of domestic violence, afraid she can't make it on her own
- A person struggling under cancer's death sentence
- A family trying to live down a personal scandal
- A trusted employee who for months has been embezzling from his or her company
- Teenagers who are spiritually hungry yet intensely aware of the peer pressure around them
- Social climbers who sit in the pews because their attendance at church might give them a leg up in the job market but for whom in their hearts envy and ambition are running wild
- A devout church leader for whom religion is losing its vitality
- A once-devoted teacher becoming disillusioned with the politics of public education
- Parishioners burning with fires of lust or smoldering with hatred's passion
- And a few for whom jealousy and unhappiness with their station in life has poisoned life's cup, making it a drink of bitterness

A mixture of these and many more are before us each time we preach.[9]

Sixth, good preachers are always conscious of the different ways people hear the gospel. According to some studies there are as many as forty-two different kinds of listeners in a congregation on Sunday morning.[10] Different people hear and conceive of the sermon in different ways. There is the rational crowd, narrative crowd, image crowd, open-ended crowd, and so forth. This means you should never doubt your own preaching style. There will always be people who will have an appreciation for the way you preach. Therefore you don't have to mimic the style of anyone else. For example, A.M.E. Bishop John Bryant and Charles Booth of the Shiloh Baptist Church in Columbus, Ohio, are great preachers. We all love to hear them preach, but even while admiring the great preachers, you must always remember that your particular style of preaching can also be heard on its own merits.

1. Some people hear better through rational, discursive argument.

There are many parishioners and congregants who still prefer the deductive, three-point sermonic form. So when you read 1 Corinthians 13:1–13, you can feel free in outlining your sermon in a logical, rational, discursive manner. The sermon could be titled "What the World Needs Now Is Love, Sweet Love!"

1. First of all I say to you, *Love alone counts*—"If I speak in the tongues of mortals and of angels, but do not have love, I am a noisy gong or a clanging cymbal."
2. Second, I say to you, *Love alone wins*—"Love is patient; love is kind; love is not envious or boastful or arrogant or rude. It does not insist on its own way." Some try to win with something other than love. They are often heard saying, "Don't start none, and it won't be none . . . " or "I cover the ground I stand on." But love alone wins!
3. Finally, *Love alone lasts*—"Love never ends. But as for prophecies, they will come to an end; as for tongues, they will cease; as for knowledge, it will come to an end. . . . And now faith, hope, and love abide, these three: but the greatest of these is love."[11]

For some, love is simply a feeling that you feel when you feel that feeling that you never felt before. But that is hardly Christian love. Love is the most stubborn emotion in the human condition. When you love, you have something that water can't drown, fire can't burn, and the wind can't blow away. Love lasts longer than life, and it's deeper than the grave. Christian love is

1. A love of identity—you seek to identify with the situation of the other.
2. A love of sacrifice—he ain't heavy, he's my brother or sister.
3. A love of rational goodwill—where you treat people in a manner that's best for them.

2. Some people hear better through narrative even when the narrative is constructed from one's exegesis.

Matthew 27:32 reads, "As they went out, they came upon a man from Cyrene named Simon; they compelled this man to carry his cross." Through your exegesis you reconstruct the story of how this man came to be at this particular place at this particular time. The title of your sermon could be "Serving God in Surprising Ways."

Here we have a devout Jew of the Dispersion, from North Africa, on his way to Jerusalem for one of the annual feasts. Simon had no idea he would run into this crucifixion entourage on its way to Calvary. But life is filled with unexpectedness. Just as this was true for Simon, it is also true with us. Try as you might to prepare for it, there are just some things in this life for which you cannot get ready. But even in the unexpected things of life we can encounter the unfolding purposes of God.

Moreover, Simon demonstrates for us that you can be a blessing to others and not know it. Pressed into service by an unsuspecting solider, Simon no doubt thought he was being forced to carry the cross of a common criminal consigned to the worst possible death. He had no idea whose cross he was picking up that day. He had no idea he was helping your Lord and my savior—Matthew's Messiah, Mark's Anointed One, Luke's Horn of Salvation, and John's Sweet Redeemer.

Finally, this text demonstrates for us that there are unseen benefits in things we are made to do. How many times have you heard people say, "No one makes me do anything." But there are unseen benefits in things we are made to do. Many take pride in the fact that Simon was from North Africa, but they seem not to realize that the Roman authorities made him pick up that cross. Though forced into helping Jesus, when Simon picked up that cross he became an unwitting copartner in God's eternal scheme of redemption. His name went down in the annals of history as helping Jesus in his dying hour. He became the envy of twelve legions of angels perched on the balcony of the upper deep in glory, just waiting for a chance to help Jesus. There are unseen benefits in things we are made to do. We serve God sometimes in surprising ways. Sometimes like Simon we serve God when we are forced to say yes, and sometimes like Rosa Parks we serve God when we can't help but say no. But we one and all serve God in surprising ways.[12]

3. Some hear better through images and metaphors.

For example, if you are preaching on fear you can use the image of the scarecrow in the field.

A scarecrow was placed in a field of ripening strawberries to keep predatory birds away. Hungry birds lined the fence, craving those strawberries, but fear kept them from diving in to take their fill. Two blackbirds flew in out of nowhere and landed on the scarecrow. "Oh, no," said the birds on the fence. "Don't you see that man?" "What man?" replied the blackbirds. "This is not a man. This is a scarecrow put here to scare you. If you can just get over being afraid, you can come into this field and get all the strawberries you want." The bold blackbirds immediately dove into the field of strawberries. I say to you today, if you can just get over being afraid, God has a ripening field of strawberries waiting just for you. If you can just get over that thing that has been put in your view to scare you, God has some wonderful things waiting for you.

The story of an individual can also have a powerful impact on the listening congregation.

Former first lady Laura Bush lived in fear throughout her early public life that a driving accident she had as a teenager in her Texas hometown would eventually return to haunt her. Mrs. Bush accidentally ran through a red light, hitting another car broadside. The young man driving the other car was killed. Mrs. Bush always lived in fear, especially after marrying into a prominent political family, that one day this terrible secret would become known. Overcoming her fears, she was able to tell the story to a *New York Times* reporter many years later.

4. The image of a biblical scene can also help the preacher to tell a powerful story.

The wilderness scene in the opening prologue of Mark's Gospel tells a powerful story about the importance of the wilderness in the lives of the people of faith (Mark 1:1–13).

Put before them a biblical image that has theological significance. Preach the sermon by returning to that image time and time again.

Owing to their past travels and travails there developed among the Israelites a wilderness theology. The wilderness became for them a place not only of preparation but also of repentance. It was not only a place where one prepared for new goals and achievement in God; it was also the place where one got right with God. Too many are all to eager to get "ready," but we must also get "right."

The wilderness is the place where you truly come to understand that you cannot make this journey by yourselves. It contains wild beasts and angels—adversaries of God but also agents of God. It is a place of danger and divinity. A place of warning and promise. The warning is that you will be tested. The promise is that you will be ministered to when the battle is over.

Seventh, one becomes a better preacher by developing a keen insight into the human situation. Good preachers are inquisitive. I didn't say nosy, but inquisitive. One takes every experience, every opportunity that life presents to see God's hand and to name God's presence in the world. You don't need a book of illustrations in order to be an effective preacher. You need the twin powers of observation and imagination. God and the works of God are all around us; we have only to observe them and assign them a place in our sanctified imagination. I recall some years ago feeling saddened and dejected when I discovered that I would not be able to graduate with my PhD degree the year I thought I would. Told by my advisor that my dissertation needed a little more work, I simply could not muster the energy to go back to the research right away. Feeling the weight of the world on my shoulders, I got out of my car on a cold winter day and headed into my office at the New Brunswick Theological Seminary where I was an assistant professor. To my surprise, I looked up and saw a squirrel standing in the snow with a chocolate chip cookie in his front paws. I thought, if God remembers that a squirrel needs breakfast surely God has not forgotten me. I walked on into the building with renewed energy and encouragement. The receptionist at the desk greeted me with a warm good morning and asked how I was feeling. I said to her, "I'm feeling just fine because a squirrel just preached a sermon to me." Good illustrations come to us out of the real situations of life.

Finally, a word from Scripture. Second Timothy 4:2–5 says,

Proclaim the message; be persistent whether the time is favorable or unfavorable; convince, rebuke, and encourage, with the utmost patience in teaching. For the time is coming when people will not put up with sound doctrine, but having itching ears, they will accumulate for themselves teachers to suit their own desires, and will turn away from listening to the truth and wander away to myths.

As for you, always be sober, endure suffering, do the work of an evangelist, carry out your ministry fully.

Such are the makings of an effective preacher who desires to get better at the foolishness of preaching.

Appendix A

Oral Formulas in the Black Culture

Oral formulas are made up of clichés, colloquial expressions, adages, aphorisms, maxims, and mottos. They can also be made up of well-known hymns, poems, and other expressions that signify. The one-liners listed below are spoken so often and so freely that they become a part of the black way of being in the world. Many sermons are peppered with them, and the black congregation usually immediately understands the sense in which they are being employed.

1. You don't miss your water until your well runs dry.
2. A hard head makes a soft behind.
3. A fool and his money soon part company.
4. Your mouth is going to get you in worlds of trouble.
5. Behind every dark cloud there's a silver lining.
6. If you make your bed hard, you have to sleep in it.
7. Bought wisdom is the best kind.
8. The darkest hour is just before day.
9. God is good all the time; all the time God is good.
10. You can lead a horse to the water, but you can't make him drink.
11. A man works from sun to sun, but a woman's work is never done.
12. The hand that rocks the cradle is the hand that rules the world.
13. A day late and a dollar short.
14. The early bird catches the worm.
15. A bird in the hand is better than two in the bush.
16. A cat has nine lives.
17. Don't look a gift horse in the mouth.
18. Couldn't hit him in the behind with a red apple.

19. God don't love ugly, and he ain't stuck on beauty.
20. Can two walk together except they be agreed?
21. Beauty is only skin deep, but ugly is to the bone.
22. It must be jelly, 'cause jam don't shake that way.
23. What goes around comes around.
24. The proof of the pudding is in the eating.
25. It hasn't been this cold since the day Roberta died.
26. She is stepping in high cotton.
27. He is sharp as a tack and twice as rusty.
28. Absence makes the heart grow fonder.
29. If you play, you pay.
30. I was on him like the letter "d" in the word "dead"—I had him covered on both ends.
31. Too many cooks spoil the broth.
32. If you study long, you study wrong.
33. If you can't stand the heat, get the hell out of the kitchen.
34. I cover the ground I stand on.
35. Don't let your mouth write a check your behind can't cash.
36. I was born at night, but it wasn't last night.
37. A liar can't tarry in his sight.
38. A still tongue makes a wise head.
39. No news is good news.
40. To each his own.
41. Beauty is in the eye of the beholder.
42. What's good for the goose is good for the gander.
43. It takes one to know one.
44. Birds of a feather flock together.
45. It's a mighty poor dog that won't wag his own tail.
46. Let sleeping dogs lie.
47. If a dog brings a bone, he'll carry one.
48. Two wrongs don't make a right.
49. Do unto others as you would have them do unto you.
50. Every tub must stand on its own bottom.
51. Cleanliness is next to godliness.
52. We're going to put the big pot in the little pot.
53. She's sitting pretty.
54. The same snake that bit me once won't bite me twice.
55. Don't loan your money to kinfolk and friends.
56. Haste makes waste.
57. You couldn't give it to me on a silver platter.
58. Root hog, or die poor.

59. Wild horses couldn't stop me.
60. Don't throw the baby out with the bath water.
61. You've got the cart before the horse.
62. You closed the door after the horse was out of the barn.
63. It's a mighty long road that does not have a turn in it somewhere.
64. All good things must come to an end.
65. If I don't see you again in a thousand years, it'll be too soon.
66. I used to not know you.
67. Forever and a day.
68. When hell freezes over.
69. Not as long as heaven is happy and hell is hot.
70. When pigs fly.
71. It's too good to be true.
72. You can't take it with you.
73. You can choose your friends, but you can't choose your kinfolk.
74. Feed your enemies with a long handle spoon.
75. You can't borrow your way out of debt.
76. You're not the only pebble on the beach.
77. One monkey doesn't stop the whole show.
78. Give me back my business.
79. The blacker the berry, the sweeter the juice.
80. This is A and B conversation, so C (see) your way out of it.
81. You can't have your cake and eat it too.
82. Do it and die.
83. A stitch in time saves nine.
84. Still water runs deep.
85. No mother wit and very little father wit.
86. A face only a mother could love.
87. I need it like I need another hole in my head.
88. He's a chip off the old block.
89. The apple doesn't fall too far from the tree.
90. Six in one hand and half a dozen in the other.
91. There's no fool like an old fool.
92. He's still wet behind the ears.
93. Stuck on stupid and parked in dumb.
94. Don't be a fair-weather friend.
95. All that glitters is not gold.
96. There's a fungus among us.
97. My money was funny, my change was strange, and my credit couldn't get it!
98. I don't play the dozen.

99. If you're feeling froggy, you can hop [an invitation to fisticuffs].
100. He may not come when you want him, but he'll be right on time [providence of God].
101. He's as sure for hell as a dime is for a ginny.
102. Spare the rod and spoil the child.
103. She's trying to make a dollar out of fifteen cents.
104. Robbing Peter to pay Paul.
105. Favor ain't fair.
106. Let the door hit you where the good Lord split you.
107. He's in a melluva hess [hell of a mess].
108. Garbage in, garbage out.
109. Buying what you want and begging for what you need.
110. You got diamonds in your back; you look good going [good-bye and good riddance].

Appendix B

"What Are You Afraid Of?"

(Matt. 25:14–30)

" 'So I was afraid, and I went and hid your talent in the ground. Here you have what is yours.' "
                                                     —Matthew 25:25

In the parable before us this morning there are three people on the receiving end of money. One is given five talents, another is given two talents, and a third is given one talent. In biblical times a talent was a measure of money. According to some estimates, one talent was the equivalent of fifteen years of a laborer's wages. As you can see, all three people in the text have been given a substantial sum of money for the purpose of trading with it profitably in their master's absence. The one who received five talents went immediately and put his master's money to work. The one who received two talents went immediately and put his master's money to work. But the one who received one talent dug a hole and buried his master's money in the ground. After a long time the master of those slaves returned and asked them to give an account of what they had done with their money. Those who had put their money to good use were happy to make their report. You don't mind making your report when you have done your best. The one who received five talents said to his master, "I put your money to good use, and I have increased my talents to ten." His master said to him, "Well done, good and trustworthy slave." The one who received two talents said, "I put your money to good use, and I have increased my talents to four." His master said to him, "Well done, good and trustworthy slave."

I hope by now you can get some sense of the movement of this text. It does not matter how much or how little the slaves were given. As long as they did their best and put their money to work, they received the same words of commendation from the master. But when it was time for the one who had been given one talent to report to his master, he began scratching where he was not itching and grinning when nothing was funny. Instead of moving towards his master he began to do a back step away from his master. He said to his master, "I knew that you were a harsh man, reaping where you did not sow, and gathering where you did not scatter seed; so I was afraid, and went and hid your talent in the ground. Here you have what is yours." Fear caused him to act in an irresponsible manner with that which had been entrusted to him for a season.

Many of us respond to this parable by saying, "Oh, how silly, how foolish, how irrational, how unreasonable for him to be afraid simply because he had been given only one talent." But in reality we should not be too harsh on this person with one talent, for Jesus intends for us to see ourselves in this man. This person with one talent is us, and we are that person. For we are all afraid of something. It may yet to be revealed publicly. It may yet reside in the inner recesses of our hearts, but we are all afraid of something just like this person in the text. Something that keeps us from being all that God would have us to be. Something that keeps us from coming to full maturity in the faith. What are we afraid of? Some people are afraid of their past. There is some unfortunate incident, some grave error, some mistake in judgment, some word or deed spoken or done that they wish a thousand times they could call back. So they live in fear hoping such things in their past will never see the light of day. I remind us here not to be too critical of people when skeletons from their closet are revealed, for it is Henry Wadsworth Longfellow who reminds us that "all houses wherein men have lived and died are haunted houses." Yes, we all live in haunted houses, and we never know when a ghost from our past is coming home to haunt us.

Some people live in fear of the present. People who have come up the rough side of the mountain. People for whom life has not been easy. People who have born their burdens in the heat of the day. People who have worked hard to get where they are in life. People who have struggled to pay for a home, sacrificed to send children to school, and saved to have something in retirement. These people, if not careful, can find themselves fearful of the present, fearful that all they've managed to gain could be lost in an instant. And in this day of cutbacks, layoffs, pink slips, and reductions in force such fears are not so unreasonable. Langston Hughes in his poem *Mother to Son* spoke for many when he said, "Life for me ain't been no crystal stair."

Then there are those who fear the future. This is especially true of senior citizens as they come to the twilight of their days. Even those who have trusted God all their lives can at times find themselves fearing what tomorrow may bring: Lord will my health hold out? Will I be able to stay in my right mind? Will I become a burden to my children? Will they have to put me in a nursing home? Will they have to break my door down and find me sprawled out on the floor unnoticed and unattended? God, what will my end be? We are all afraid of something, and at times that fear causes us to act irresponsibly with that which God has entrusted to each of us. We fear exposure. We fear loneliness. We fear sickness. We fear disease. We fear terror. We fear death. We are afraid of not being able to handle the threat of a special situation. We fear that something will come up in our lives at a time when we are most vulnerable and least able to handle it. Mark Twain is supposed to have said that ninety percent of the stuff we worry about never happens. Ponder that for a moment: Ninety percent of the stuff we worry about never happens. The Protestant reformer John Calvin said the human mind is a factory of fears. Yes, our minds just crank out stuff for us to be afraid of. We are all afraid of something.

That which we fear will eventually manifest itself in our lives somehow. Sometimes what we fear shows up in our lives as a loss of direction. The person with five talents moved out in one direction. The person with two talents moved out in another. However, the person with one talent moved downward. He dug a hole and buried his master's money in the ground. Fear caused him to lose his sense of direction. How many times have you heard people say they aspire to reach certain goals? There are certain things in this life they'd like to achieve. "But," they say, "if I go in this direction, it might not work out. If I try my hand in this area, I might fail miserably. Or, if I take out in another direction, I might be humiliated." So, because of fear they lose all sense of direction and end up going nowhere. Sometimes what we fear shows up in our lives as a loss of verve and vitality. Our get-up-and-go has gotten up and gone. There is no fire in the belly. There is no can-do spirit. We find ourselves stuck in a rut, unable to move in any direction. The great gospel singer Mahalia Jackson used to sing a song that said, "Standing here wondering which way to go, so much confusion in this world below." So oft times when we lose our zeal and zest for life, we find ourselves standing at the crossroads wondering which way to go. We feel that each time we try to move forward the dead hand of the past slaps us back.

Sometimes that which we fear shows up in our lives as an over-whelming sense of inadequacy. We say to God, "God, when I look around and see how you have blessed others—how much they have, how much they know, and where they have been—I really feel that you did not give me all that I need to make it in this life." When we think such thoughts, an overwhelming sense of inadequacy can overtake us. Feelings of inadequacy can eventually lead to feelings of jealousy and envy, all brought on, in large part, by fear. While I do not have all of the answers to our fears, I do want to speak to the fear that keeps us from using all that God has given us in this life. Fear can prevent us from putting to use what God has distinctly granted to us. I suppose this person with one talent was doing all right until he remembered there was a person out there with two times as much. And I need not tell you what he said the day he remembered there was a person out there with five times as much. Whenever we start to think of ourselves as little and insignificant, we are headed down "mess up" road. There is not a person living to whom God has not given something. You may not be able to sing like an angel, and you may not be able to preach like Paul, but God has given you something to function with in this life. And God is looking to you to make your contribution to the human situation. Moreover, there is one thing no one can beat you doing: your best! When you have done your best, that's all God requires.

Also, God never gives anything everything. You have only to look at nature to know this is true. Look at the peacock strutting and preening in full plumage. You could look at that proud bird and say, "My goodness, God gave the peacock everything." But just keep looking. Look past that sun-crowned head. Look past the colorful tail feathers. Look past that mighty strut, and look down at those feet. Ah, you will see some of the dirtiest, rustiest, most scratched-up feet ever. You will then say, "No, no, God did not give the peacock everything." God always saves something for you and for me. God has given you something to function with in this life.

And may I say to you, we could come to such peace and contentment in life if we could convince ourselves that we are where we are supposed to be and that we are doing what we are supposed to be doing. I am reminded here of a story where a man took his son to a parcel of land he owned and told him to chop down the weeds at the corner of the lot. While the little boy was chopping weeds, he noticed that some businessmen scouting out land nearby for possible development had gotten confused about the best way to get back to the city. They yelled across the way to the little boy, "Hey kid, which road leads back to the city?" The little boy yelled back, "The city is that way." Confused as to the location of the city himself, the boy quickly yelled out once more, "Hey stop! I'm sorry! The city is the other way!" One of the businessmen said to the others in the group, "Let's not trouble the little boy any further; he is clearly lost." The little boy replied, "No, I'm not lost. I'm where I'm supposed to be. My father told me to work this part of the field." "But," said the businessman, "You don't even know how to get to the city." The little boy said, "That's because I'm not going to the city. But I'm not lost. I am where I'm supposed to be." We, too, could come to such peace of mind if we could just recognize that we are where we are supposed to be and we are doing what we are supposed to be doing.

May I also say that this person with one talent focused too much on what he did not have and not enough on what the master had given to him. He thought to himself that he wouldn't mind working with his one talent if he just didn't have to be around others who had been given so much. If he could be in a different environment, a different milieu, he would feel so much better about his limited gift. But this person with one talent was not being true to life. There will never come a time in life when all things are just like you'd like for them to be. If you are waiting for your life to be just right, you never will do anything with what God has given to you. In this life we have to learn to play the hand that life deals us. We would all like a hand filled with jacks, kings, and queens. But the truth of the matter is that someone has to have some threes, fours, and fives. When you get a bad hand, learn how to keep a straight face. Take courage in the fact that the God you serve is in charge of the shuffle, and while it may not be the hand you prefer, it is a playable hand.

If you are here this morning and you have hidden your talent in the earth, go and dig it up! Go now! Go at once! Go as you are! Go now while it is still day. Go before the hour of judgment strikes. Go before the master returns. Go and use what God has given you! Use it to the glory of God, for the betterment of humankind, and for the up-building of the kingdom. And the people of God said, Amen.

Notes

PREFACE

1. Karl Barth, *The Word of God and the Word of Man*, trans. Douglas Horton (Gloucester, MA: Peter Smith, 1978), 119–20.

2. Paul S. Wilson, *Setting Words on Fire: Putting God at the Center of the Sermon* (Nashville: Abingdon Press, 2008), 149.

CHAPTER 2: BLACK PREACHING AND WHITE HOMILETICS

1. Richard Eslinger, *A New Hearing: Living Options in Homiletic Method* (Nashville: Abingdon Press, 1987), 11.

2. David Buttrick, *Homiletic* (Philadelphia: Fortress Press, 1987), 469.

3. Leander Keck, *The Bible in the Pulpit* (Nashville: Abingdon Press, 1978), 15.

4. For comments by Lischer, see David V. Biema and Nadia Mustafa, "How Much Does Preaching Matter?" *Time*, 17 September 2001, quote on 55; and for Wilson, see Cleophus J. LaRue, *The Heart of Black Preaching* (Louisville: Westminster John Knox Press, 1999), back cover.

5. Stephen Farris, *Preaching That Matters* (Louisville, KY: Westminster John Knox Press, 1998), 18–19.

6. Cited in David Van Biema, "America's Best: Spirit Raiser," *Time*, 17 September 2001, 53.

7. David James Randolph, *The Renewal of Preaching* (Philadelphia: Fortress Press, 1969), 2.

8. Keck, *Bible in the Pulpit*, 40.

9. Mechal Sobel, *The World They Made Together: Black and White Values in Eighteenth-Century Virginia* (Princeton, NJ: Princeton University Press, 1987), 11. See also Nathan O. Hatch, *The Democratization of American Christianity* (New Haven, CT: Yale University Press, 1989); and Donald G. Mathews, *Religion in the Old South* (Chicago: University of Chicago Press, 1977).

10. James W. Cox, ed., *The Twentieth-Century Pulpit* (Nashville: Abingdon Press, 1978), 115–23. Justo Gonzalez rightly notes in his critique of this work that a

rapid glance at the list of contributors shows that they are all male and that almost all of them are white. See Gonzalez, *Liberation Preaching* (Nashville: Abingdon Press, 1980), 46. Had the editor sought a more inclusive list of black preachers and sermons, he could have read the works of such nineteenth- and early twentieth-century greats as Alexander Crummell, *The Greatness of Christ and Other Sermons* (New York: Thomas Whittaker, 1882); *Africa and America: Addresses and Discourses* (New York: Negro Universities Press, 1891); Carter G. Woodson, ed., *The Works of Francis J. Grimke*, Special Collections, Princeton Theological Seminary, 1942; J. W. Hood, *The Negro in the Christian Pulpit* (Raleigh, NC: Edwards, Broughton, & Co., 1884); C. S. Smith, *Sermons Delivered by Bishop Daniel A. Payne* (Nashville: Publishing House of the A.M.E. Sunday School Union, 1888); and Theodore S. Boone, "*Lord! Lord!*"*: Special Occasion Sermons and Addresses of Dr. L. K. Williams* (Nashville: Historical Commission, National Baptist Convention, Inc., 1942).

11. The notable exceptions are Keith D. Miller, *Voice of Deliverance: The Language of Martin Luther King Jr. and Its Sources* (New York: Free Press, 1992); Richard Lischer, *The Preacher King: Martin Luther King Jr. and the Word That Moved America* (New York: Oxford University Press, 1995); Richard L. Eslinger, *The Web of Preaching* (Nashville: Abingdon Press, 2002); and L. Susan Bond, *Contemporary African American Preaching: Diversity in Theory and Style* (St. Louis: Chalice Press, 2003). Stephen Farris, Leonora Tisdale, and Paul Scott Wilson, among others, have sought to incorporate black preachers and homileticians into their works on preaching.

12. Even books on great preaching published in the twentieth century were slow about including the sermons of prominent, historical African American preachers. Clyde E. Fant Jr., and William M. Pinson Jr., eds. (*Twenty Centuries of Great Preaching: An Encyclopedia of Preaching* [Waco: Word Books, 1971]), cite the names of John Jasper and Martin Luther King Jr. in their multivolume set. Warren W. Wiersbe, ed. (*Treasury of the World's Great Sermons* [Grand Rapids: Kregel Publications, 1977]), published the sermons of no recognizable black preachers from the early beginnings of Christianity through the twentieth century. Not even a sermon by Martin Luther King Jr. was able to make his list. To Wiersbe's credit, he widened his circle and came in later years to have an appreciation for black preaching with the publication of his coauthored conversations on preaching with African American pastor E. K. Bailey. See E. K. Bailey and Warren Wiersbe, *Preaching in Black and White: What We Can Learn from Each Other* (Grand Rapids: Zondervan, 2003).

13. Fred Craddock, *As One without Authority* (Enid, OK: Phillips University Press, 1974), 53–54.

14. Ibid., 55.

15. Ibid., 90.

16. Buttrick, *Homiletic*, 83–96.

17. See Cheryl Sanders's essay "Preaching with Passion," in *Power in the Pulpit: How America's Most Effective Black Preachers Prepare Their Sermons*, ed. Cleophus J. LaRue (Louisville, KY: Westminster John Knox Press, 2002), 117–28.

18. Karl Barth, *The Word of God and the Word of Man* (Gloucester: Peter Smith, 1978), 114.

19. For a more detailed analysis of the call-and-response dynamic in the black worship setting see Evans E. Crawford and Thomas Troeger, *The Hum: Call and Response in African American Preaching* (Nashville: Abingdon Press, 1995).

20. Eugene L. Lowry, *The Homiletical Plot: The Sermon as Narrative Art Form* (Atlanta: John Knox Press, 1978).

21. Paul Scott Wilson, *The Four Pages of the Sermon: A Guide to Biblical Preaching* (Nashville: Abingdon Press, 1999).

22. Thomas G. Long, *The Witness of Preaching* (Louisville, KY: Westminster/ John Knox Press, 1989).

23. Charles L. Campbell, *Preaching Jesus: New Directions for Homiletics in Hans Frei's Postliberal Theology* (Grand Rapids: Wm. B. Eerdmans Publishing Co., 1997).

24. Gerhard O. Forde, *Theology Is for Proclamation* (Minneapolis: Fortress Press, 1990); and Edward Farley, *Practicing Gospel: Unconventional Thoughts on the Church's Ministry* (Louisville, KY: Westminster John Knox Press, 2003).

25. James J. Buckley and David S. Yeago, eds., *Knowing the Triune God: The Work of the Spirit in the Practices of the Church* (Grand Rapids: Wm. B. Eerdmans Publishing Co., 2001), 49–93.

26. Wardell J. Payne, ed., *Directory of African American Religious Bodies* (Washington DC: Howard University Press, 1991), 21–47, 199–216; and Larry G. Murphy, J. Gordon Melton, and Gary L. Ward, eds., *Encyclopedia of African American Religions* (New York: Garland Publishing, 1993), xx. The *Encyclopedia* lists some 341 black religious organizations.

27. Anthony B. Pinn, *The Black Church in the Post-Civil Rights Era* (Maryknoll, NY: Orbis Books, 2002), 35.

28. C. Eric Lincoln and Lawrence H. Mamiya, *The Black Church in the African American Experience* (Durham, NC: Duke University Press, 1990), 1.

29. Proctor's ideas are discussed by Susan Bond in *Contemporary African American Preaching: Diversity in Theory and Style* (St. Louis: Chalice Press, 2003), 44.

30. Samuel D. Proctor, *Preaching About Crises in the Community* (Philadelphia: Westminster Press, 1988); *The Certain Sound of the Trumpet: Crafting a Sermon of Authority* (Valley Forge, PA: Judson Press, 1994); *The Substance of Things Hoped For: A Memoir of African-American Faith* (New York: G. P. Putnam's Sons, 1995).

31. Samuel D. Proctor and William D. Watley, *Sermons from the Black Pulpit* (Valley Forge, PA: Judson Press, 1984).

32. Gardner C. Taylor, *How Shall They Preach* (Elgin, IL: Progressive Baptist Publishing House, 1977).

33. James Forbes Jr., *The Holy Spirit and Preaching* (Nashville: Abingdon Press, 1989).

34. William B. McClain, "African-American Preaching," in *The Renewal of Sunday Worship*, ed. Robert E. Webber (Nashville: StarSong, 1993), 315–19.

35. James Earl Massey, *The Responsible Pulpit* (Anderson, IN: Warner Press, 1974), 101–11.

36. Henry Mitchell, *Black Preaching* (San Francisco: Wm. B. Eerdmans Publishing Co., 1970); and *Experience and Celebration in Preaching* (Nashville: Abingdon Press, 1990).

37. Henry H. Mitchell, "African-American Preaching," in *Concise Encyclopedia of Preaching*, ed. William H. Willimon and Richard Lischer (Louisville, KY: Westminster John Knox Press, 1995), 3–9.

38. Crawford and Troeger, *The Hum.*

39. Ibid. 13.

40. Cleophus J. LaRue, *The Heart of Black Preaching* (Louisville, KY: Westminster John Knox Press, 2000).

41. An oft-told tale is the story of the King of Benares, who entertained himself and his court by putting an elephant in the midst of half-a-dozen blind men and asked them to tell him what it was. One got hold of the trunk and said it was a rope; one, the leg and said it was a tree; one, the ear and said it was a winnowing fan—and so on. Discussions about religious phenomena that have myriad characteristics are at best a discussion of blind people touching different parts of an elephant. See Lesslie Newbigin, *The Finality of Christ* (London: SCM Press, 1969), 16–17.

42. For additional works on black preaching and works written by black preachers see Kelly Miller Smith, *Social Crisis Preaching* (Macon, GA: Mercer University Press, 1983); Olin P. Moyd, *The Sacred Art: Preaching and Theology in the African American Tradition* (Valley Forge, PA: Judson Press, 1995); Miles Jones, *Preaching Papers: The Hampton and Virginia Union Lectures* (New York: MLK Fellows Press, 1995); Warren H. Stewart, *Interpreting God's Word in Black Preaching* (Valley Forge, PA: Judson Press, 1984); Samuel D. Proctor, *The Certain Sound of the Trumpet: Crafting a Sermon of Authority* (Valley Forge, PA: Judson Press, 1994); Gardner C. Taylor, *How Shall They Preach* (Elgin, IL: Progressive Baptist Publishing House, 1977); James H. Harris, *Preaching Liberation* (Minneapolis: Fortress Press, 1993); Massey, *The Responsible Pulpit*; Bruce A. Rosenberg, *Can These Bones Live? The Art of the American Folk Preacher* (New York: Oxford University Press, 1970); Mitchell, *Experience and Celebration*; Frank Thomas, *They Like to Never Quit Praisin' God: The Role of Celebration in Preaching* (Cleveland: Pilgrim Press, 1997); Cleophus J. LaRue, *Heart of Black Preaching;* and *Power in the Pulpit: How America's Most Effective Black Preachers Prepare Their Sermons* (Louisville, KY: Westminster/John Knox Press, 2002); Gerald L. Davis, *I Got the Word in Me and I Can Sing It, You Know: A Study of the Performed African American Sermon* (Philadelphia: University of Pennsylvania Press, 1985); Bettye Collier-Thomas, *Daughters of Thunder: Black Women Preachers and Their Sermons, 1850–1979* (San Francisco: Jossey-Bass Publishers, 1998); Katie G. Cannon, *Teaching Preaching: Isaac Rufus Clark and Black Sacred Rhetoric* (New York:

Continuum, 2002); Marvin McMickle, *Preaching to the Black Middle Class* (Valley Forge, PA: Judson Press, 2000); and Teresa Fry Brown, *Weary Throats and New Songs: Black Women Preaching God's Word* (Nashville: Abingdon Press, 2003). For two excellent pieces where blacks and whites are in conversation with one another see Bailey and Wiersbe, *Preaching in Black and White* and Brian K. Blount and Gary W. Charles, *Preaching Mark in Two Voices* (Louisville, KY: Westminster/John Knox Press, 2002).

CHAPTER 3: PULPITS WITHOUT PURPOSE

1. The "mainline" refers to those Protestant ecclesiastical institutions that for decades have enjoyed an unofficial "establishment status" in American culture. Related terms for the mainline are "old-line" and "sideline." See Thomas C. Oden, *Turning Around the Mainline: How Renewal Movements Are Changing the Church* (Grand Rapids: Baker Books, 2006), 37–39.

2. Jackson W. Carroll, *Mainline to the Future: Congregations for the Twenty-first Century* (Louisville, KY: Westminster John Knox Press, 2000), x; and Alister E. McGrath, *The Future of Christianity* (Malden, MA: Blackwell Publishing, 2002), 40–71.

3. "Seeker churches" is defined as those churches that design their services and programs to attract those who are unchurched.

4. "Wretch" is defined as a miserable, unhappy, unfortunate person. Some have replaced it in their hymn books with the word "soul."

5. Carroll, *Mainline*, x.

6. From an unpublished paper presented at a Homiletical Feast Conference in Tampa, Florida, January 10, 2004.

7. Carroll, *Mainline*, x–xi.

8. Jonathan L. Walton, "A Cultural Analysis of the Black Electronic Church Phenomenon" (PhD dissertation, Princeton Theological Seminary, 2006). Walton has written a very telling dissertation on the black church and television.

9. Neil Postman, *Amusing Ourselves to Death: Public Discourse in the Age of Show Business* (New York: Penguin Books, 1985), 4.

10. Ibid., 114–24.

11. Stephen W. Angell, *Bishop Henry McNeal Turner and African-American Religion in the South* (Knoxville: University of Tennessee Press, 1992), 148–49.

12. Clarence E. Walker, *A Rock in a Weary Land: The African Methodist Episcopal Church during the Civil War and Reconstruction* (Baton Rouge: Louisiana State Press, 1982), 22–24.

13. Ibid.

14. Angell, *Henry McNeal Turner*, 149–50.

15. See James M. Washington, *Frustrated Fellowship: The Black Baptist Quest for Social Power* (Macon, GA: Mercer University Press, 1968).

16. Michael W. Harris, *The Rise of Gospel Blues: The Music of Thomas Andrew Dorsey in the Urban Church* (New York: Oxford University Press, 1992), 258.

17. Ibid.

18. Karl Barth as quoted in Carroll, *Mainline*, 1.

19. Ibid., 7.

20. Ibid., 9.

21. Andrew F. Walls, *The Cross-Cultural Process in Christian History* (Maryknoll, NY: Orbis Books, 2002), 8–26.

22. Ibid., 13–18.

23. Ibid., 18–25.

24. John Bright, *The Authority of the Old Testament* (Grand Rapids: Baker Book House, 1989), 162.

25. P. T. Forsyth, *Positive Preaching and the Modern Mind* (London: Independent Press, 1907), 1.

26. Paul E. Scherer, *For We Have This Treasure* (Grand Rapids: Baker Book House, 1943), 21.

27. Karl Barth, *Church Dogmatics*, vol. 4, *The Doctrine of Reconciliation* (Edinburgh: T. & T. Clark, 1956), 211–82; and Edward R. Hardy, ed., *Christology of the Later Fathers* (Philadelphia: Westminster Press, 1954), 359–70.

CHAPTER 4: THE SHAPE OF COLORED PREACHING IN THE TWENTY-FIRST CENTURY

1. Philip Jenkins, *The Next Christendom: The Coming of Global Christianity* (New York: Oxford University Press, 2002), 3.

2. Ibid., 7

3. See Cleophus J. LaRue, *The Heart of Black Preaching* (Louisville, KY: Westminster John Knox Press, 1999).

4. See Cleophus J. LaRue, "Two Ships Passing in the Night," in *What's the Matter with Preaching Today*, ed. Mike Graves (Louisville, KY: Westminster John Knox Press, 2004), 127–44.

5. O. C. Edwards, *A History of Preaching* (Nashville: Abingdon Press, 2004), 526–57, 703–30; Richard Lischer, *The Preacher King: Martin Luther King and the Word That Moved America* (New York: Oxford University Press, 1995); Keith D. Miller, *Voice of Deliverance: The Language of Martin Luther King, Jr. and Its Sources* (New York: Free Press, 1992); Susan Bond, *Contemporary African American Preaching: Diversity in Theory and Style* (St. Louis: Chalice Press, 2003); Paul Scott Wilson, *The Four Pages of the Sermon: A Guide to Biblical Preaching* (Nashville: Abingdon Press, 1999); and Gary Selby, *Martin Luther King and the Rhetoric of Freedom* (Waco, TX: Baylor University Press, 2008).

6. E. K. Bailey and Warren W. Wiersbe, *Preaching in Black and White: What We Can Learn from Each Other* (Grand Rapids: Zondervan Press, 2003); Brian K. Blount and Gary W. Charles, *Preaching Mark in Two Voices* (Louisville, KY: Westminster John Knox Press, 2002); and Evans E. Crawford and Thomas H. Troeger, *The Hum: Call and Response in African American Preaching* (Nashville: Abingdon Press, 1995).

7. Samuel D. Proctor, *The Certain Sound of the Trumpet: Crafting a Sermon of Authority* (Valley Forge, PA: Judson Press, 1994); Gardner C. Taylor, *How Shall They Preach* (Elgin, IL: Progressive Baptist Publishing House, 1977); James H. Harris, *Preaching Liberation* (Minneapolis: Fortress Press, 1995); James Forbes, *The Holy Spirit and Preaching* (Nashville: Abingdon Press, 1989); and Frank Thomas, *They Like to Never Quit Praisin' God: The Role of Celebration in Preaching* (Cleveland: Pilgrim Press, 1997).

8. Andrew F. Walls, "Christian Scholarship and the Demographic Transformation of the Church," in *Theological Literacy for the Twenty-First Century*, ed. Rodney L. Petersen and Nancy M. Rourke (Grand Rapids: Wm. B. Eerdmans Publishing Co., 2002), 171.

9. Ibid., 172

10. Jenkins, *The Next Christendom*, 2; Kwame Bediako, *Christianity in Africa* (Edinburgh: University Press/Orbis Books, 1995), 154; and John S. Mbiti, *African Religions and Philosophy* (England: Heinemann Publishers, 1992).

11. Walls, "Christian Scholarship," 173.

12. Harvey Cox, *Fire From Heaven: The Rise of Pentecostal Spirituality and the Reshaping of Religion in the Twenty-First Century* (Cambridge: Da Capo Press, 1995).

13. Walls, "Christian Scholarship," 177.

14. Ibid.

15. Ibid.

16. William H. Myers, *God's Yes Was Louder Than My No: Rethinking the African American Call to Ministry* (Grand Rapids: Wm. B. Eerdmans Publishing Co., 1994), 28. See also by Myers, *The Irresistible Urge to Preach: A Collection of African American "Call" Stories* (Atlanta: Aaron Press Publishers, 1991).

17. Gardner C. Taylor, "A Holy Pursuit," *Power in the Pulpit: How America's Most Effective Black Preachers Prepare Their Sermons*, ed. Cleophus J. LaRue (Louisville, KY: Westminster John Knox Press, 2002), 151.

18. Martin Luther King Jr., *Strength to Love* (Philadelphia: Fortress Press, 1963), 113. See also Taylor Branch, *Parting the Waters: American in the King Years 1954–63* (New York: Simon & Schuster, 1988), 162. Branch describes this as the first transcendent religious experience in King's life: "For King, the moment awakened and confirmed his belief that the essence of religion was not a grand metaphysical idea but something personal, grounded in experience—something that opened up mysteriously beyond the predicaments of human beings in their frailest and noblest moments."

CHAPTER 5: AFRICAN AMERICAN PREACHING AND THE BIBLE

1. Albert J. Raboteau, "The Black Experience in American Evangelicalism: The Meaning of Slavery," in *The Evangelical Tradition in America*, ed. Leonard I. Sweet (Macon, GA: Mercer University Press, 1984), 181.

2. Cleophus J. LaRue, *The Heart of Black Preaching* (Louisville, KY: Westminster John Knox Press, 2000), 2.

3. Ibid., 3.

4. Carl R. Holladay, "Contemporary Methods of Reading the Bible," in *The New Interpreter's Bible,* vol. 1 (Nashville: Abingdon Press, 1994), 126.

5. Ibid.

6. Ibid.

7. Keith D. Miller, *Voice of Deliverance: The Language of Martin Luther King, Jr. and Its Sources* (New York: Free Press, 1992), 23.

8. Nathan O. Hatch, *The Democratization of American Christianity* (New Haven, CT: Yale University Press, 1989), 102–6.

9. Ibid., 107.

10. LaRue, *Heart of Black Preaching,* 21–29.

11. Ibid.

12. Ibid.

13. Ibid.

14. For further reading, see Cleophus J. LaRue, ed., *Power in the Pulpit: How America's Most Effective Black Preachers Prepare Their Sermons* (Louisville, KY: Westminster John Knox Press, 2000); Samuel D. Proctor, *The Certain Sound of the Trumpet: Crafting a Sermon of Authority* (Valley Forge, PA: Judson Press, 1994); and Gardner C. Taylor, *How Shall They Preach* (Elgin, IL: Progressive Baptist Publishing House, 1977).

CHAPTER 6: IMAGINATION AND THE EXEGETICAL EXERCISE

1. Gardner C. Taylor, *How Shall They Preach* (Elgin, IL: Progressive Baptist Publishing House, 1977), 60.

2. Fred B. Craddock, *As One without Authority* (Enid, OK: Phillips University Press, 1974), 77.

3. *Dragnet* was a television police show that aired in the 1960s and 1970s. The lead character, Sgt. Joe Friday, played by Jack Webb, questioned his potential witnesses with the same admonition each week—"The facts, ma'am, nothing but the facts."

4. John H. Leith, *From Generation to Generation: The Renewal of the Church according to Its Own Theology and Practice* (Louisville, KY: Westminster/John Knox Press, 1990), 89.

5. Taylor, *How Shall They Preach,* 58.

6. Samuel D. Proctor, *The Certain Sound of the Trumpet: Crafting a Sermon of Authority* (Valley Forge, PA: Judson Press, 1994); Thomas G. Long, *The Witness of Preaching* (Louisville, KY: Westminster/John Knox Press, 1989), 60–77; Paul Scott Wilson, *The Four Pages of the Sermon* (Nashville: Abingdon Press, 1999); and Ronald J. Allen, *Interpreting the Gospel: An Introduction to Preaching* (St. Louis: Chalice Press, 1998), 119–50.

7. LaRue, *Power in the Pulpit,* 149–50.

8. Ibid.

9. Garrett Green, *Imagining God: Theology and the Religious Imagination* (San Francisco: Harper & Row, 1987), 51.

10. Ibid.

CHAPTER 7: WHY BLACK PREACHERS STILL LOVE ARTFUL
LANGUAGE

1. John McWhorter, *Doing Our Own Thing: The Degradation of Language and Music and Why We Should, Like Care* (New York: Gotham Books, 2003), 35, 67.

2. Ibid., xvii.

3. Ibid.

4. Ibid., xix–xxiii.

5. Ibid., xxiv. In this instance McWhorter is referring to "spoken language" as unadorned talk, and he draws a distinction between talking and speaking. Unadorned talk is hardly what is being spoken in black pulpits on Sunday mornings.

6. Ibid., 51–52.

7. Ralph C. Wood, *Contending for the Faith: The Church's Engagement with Culture* (Waco, TX: Baylor University Press, 2003), 172.

8. Bruce A. Rosenberg, *Can These Bones Live? The Art of the American Folk Preacher* (Chicago: University of Illinois Press, 1970), 39.

9. Albert J. Raboteau, *A Fire in the Bones: Reflections on African-American Religious History* (Boston: Beacon Press, 1995), 141. According to Raboteau, this style of preaching originated in the prayer meetings and revivals of the rural South, but it has long since spread west and north to the cities. It remains popular among literate and sophisticated congregations alike.

10. Ibid.

11. Eugene Genovese, *Roll Jordan Roll: The World the Slaves Made* (New York: Vintage Books, 1976), 258.

12. Raboteau, *A Fire in the Bones: Reflections on African-American Religious History* (Boston: Beacon Press, 1995), 141; Eileen Southern and Josephine Wright, eds., *African American Traditions in Song, Sermon, Tale, and Dance, 1600s–1920: An Annotated Bibliography of Literature, Collections, and Artworks* (New York: Greenwood Press, 1990), xxxv; and Stephen W. Angell, *Bishop Henry McNeal Turner and African-American Religion in the South* (Knoxville: University of Tennessee Press, 1992), 21.

13. Albert J. Raboteau, *Slave Religion: The "Invisible Institution" in the Antebellum South* (New York: Oxford University Press, 1978), 236–37.

14. N. B. Woolridge, "The Slave Preacher—Portrait of a Leader," *The Journal of Negro Education,* xiv (Winter 1945): 28–37

15. Charles G. Finney, *Lectures on Revivals of Religion* (New York: Fleming H. Revell Co., 1868), 206.

16. McWhorter, *Doing Our Own Thing,* 66.

17. Ibid., 65.

18. For more information on the preaching styles of the intellectual preachers, see Gardner C. Taylor, *How Shall They Preach* (Elgin, IL: Progressive Baptist Publishing House, 1977); Manuel L. Scott, *From a Black Brother* (Nashville: Broadman Press, 1971); E. K. Bailey, *Farther in and Deeper Down* (Chicago: Moody Publishers, 2005); A. Louis Patterson, *Prerequisites for a Good Journey* (St. Louis: Hodale Press, 1994); and LaRue, *Power in the Pulpit.*

19. See Charles Adams's sermon "Faith Critiques Faith," in LaRue, ed., *Power in the Pulpit*, 18–28; William Augustus Jones, *Responsible Preaching* (Morristown, NJ: Aaron Press, 1989); Sandy Ray, *Journeying through a Jungle* (Nashville: Broadman Press, 1979); and Miles Jones, *Preaching Papers: The Hampton and Virginia Union Lectures* (New York: Martin Luther King Press, 1995).

20. For an excellent description of the whooping style of the folk preacher see "The Chanted Sermon" in Albert Raboteau's *A Fire in the Bones: Reflections on African American Religious History* (Boston: Beacon Press, 1995), 141–51; Jeff Todd Titon and C. L. Franklin, *Give Me This Mountain: Life History and Selected Sermons* (Urbana: University of Illinois Press, 1989).

21. McWhorter, *Doing Our Own Thing*, 66.

22. Ibid., 66–67.

23. Vernon Johns, "The Romance of Death" (sermon, Rankin Memorial Chapel, Howard University, May 16, 1965), 5.

24. Robert E. Hood, *Begrimed and Black: Christian Traditions on Blacks and Blackness* (Minneapolis: Fortress Press, 1994), 176–77.

25. See Cleophus J. LaRue, *The Heart of Black Preaching* (Louisville, KY: Westminster John Knox Press, 2000), 15–16.

26. Wilson J. Moses, ed., *Destiny and Race: Selected Writings, 1840–1898* (Amherst: University of Massachusetts Press, 1992), 204–5.

27. Theodore S. Boone, ed., *Lord! Lord!: Special Occasion Sermons and Addresses of Dr. L. K. Williams* (Chicago: Historical Commission, National Baptist Convention, USA, 1942), 65.

28. Shortly after delivering this lecture/sermon, one of Johns's most famous, Johns dropped dead, in a sequence his admirers swore Johns had prearranged with God. See Taylor Branch, *Parting the Waters: America in the King Years 1954–63* (New York: Simon & Schuster, 1988), 902.

29. Johns, "The Romance of Death," 7.

30. Gayraud S. Wilmore and James H. Cone, eds., *Black Theology: A Documentary History, 1966–79* (Maryknoll, NY: Orbis Books, 1979), 266.

31. "One Thankful Soul," sermon delivered by Charles Adams in Camden, New Jersey, in the early 1990s. A copy of the sermon is on file at the Media Services Center at Princeton Theological Seminary.

32. See LaRue, *Power in the Pulpit*, 70–71.

33. LaRue, *Heart of Black Preaching*, 5.

34. John H. Leith, *Introduction to the Reformed Tradition* (Atlanta: John Knox Press, 1977), 84.

35. Ibid., 87.

36. LaRue, *Heart of Black Preaching*, 10.

37. Branch, *Parting the Waters*, 902–3.

38. See Keith D. Miller, *Voice of Deliverance: The Language of Martin Luther King, Jr. and Its Sources* (New York: Free Press, 1992).

39. See appendix A for some of the oral formulas that exist in black culture and are often employed by black preachers in the preaching event.

40. Walter Ong, *Orality and Literacy*, 2nd ed. (New York: Routledge, 202), 31.

41. Catherine Ellis and Stephen Drury Smith, eds., *Say It Plain: A Century of Great African American Speeches* (New York: New Press, 2005), xi.

42. Hortense J. Spillers, "Moving on Down the Line," *American Quarterly* 40 (March 1988): 84.

43. Unpublished material from Cleo LaRue's sermon files.

44. Mahalia Jackson had heard the speech often enough to shout out to King, "Tell 'em about the dream, Martin," when his memory temporarily faltered at the March on Washington in 1963. See Greil Marcus, *The Shape of Things to Come* (New York: Farrar, Straus, Giroux, 2006), 32.

45. Branch, *Parting the Waters*, 882.

46. Ibid., 881.

47. Terry Muck and Paul Robbins, "The Sweet Torture of Sunday Morning: An Interview with Gardner C. Taylor," *Leadership Magazine* 17 (Summer Quarter 1984): 16–29; Robert M. Franklin, *Another Day's Journey: Black Churches Confronting the American Crisis* (Minneapolis: Fortress Press, 1997), 67–72.

48. Franklin, *Another Day's Journey,* 71; See also James H. Cone, "Sanctification, Liberation, and Black Worship," *Theology Today*, July 1978, 139–52.

49. James H. Harris, *The Word Made Plain: The Power and Promise of Preaching* (Minneapolis: Fortress Press, 2004), 53.

50. See LaRue, *More Power in the Pulpit.*

CHAPTER 8: ON THE PREPARATION AND DELIVERY OF SERMONS

1. Thomas G. Long, *The Witness of Preaching* (Louisville, KY: Westminster John Knox Press, 1989); Eugene Lowry, *The Homiletical Plot: The Sermon as Narrative Art Form* (Atlanta: John Knox Press, 1980); and Ronald Allen, *Interpreting the Gospel: An Introduction to Preaching* (Anderson, IN: Christian Board of Publication, 1999); and Paul S. Wilson, *The Four Pages of the Sermon: A Guide to Biblical Preaching* (Nashville: Abingdon Press, 1999).

2. Harry Emerson Fosdick believed that every sermon should have for its main business the solving of some problem—a vital important problem, puzzling minds, burdening consciences, distracting lives. Any sermon that tackled a real problem could not be altogether uninteresting. See Fosdick's "What Is the Matter with Preaching?" in *What is the Matter with Preaching Today?* ed. Tom Graves (Louisville, KY: Westminster John Knox Press, 2004), 8.

3. See Leonora Tisdale's *Preaching as Local Theology and Folk Art* (Minneapolis: Augsburg Fortress Press, 1997). Tisdale has argued for some time for a method that takes congregational exegesis more seriously and does not leave it to the biblical text alone to speak to all situations. See also James R. Nieman and Thomas G. Rogers, *Preaching to Every Pew: Cross-Cultural Strategies* (Minneapolis, MN: Fortress Press, 2001).

4. Barbara Brown Taylor, "Bothering God," in *Birthing the Sermon: Women Preachers and the Creative Process*, ed Jana Childers (St. Louis: Chalice Press, 2001), 154.

5. Fred Craddock, *As One without Authority* (Enid, OK: Phillips University Press, 1974), 77–97.

6. See Wilson, *Four Pages.*

7. See H. Beecher Hicks Jr., "Bones, Sinew, Flesh, and Blood Coming to Life," in *Inside the Sermon: Thirteen Preachers Discuss Their Methods of Preparing Messages,* ed. Richard Allen Bodey (Grand Rapids: Baker Book House, 1990), 111.

8. Ibid.

9. Ibid.

10. See William Willimon, "The Lectionary: Assessing the Gains and the Losses in a Homiletical Revolution," *Theology Today* 58 (October 2001): 333–41.

11. See James Earl Massey, *Designing the Sermon: Order and Movement in Preaching* (Nashville, TN: Abingdon Press, 1980); Samuel Dewitt Proctor, *The Certain Sound of the Trumpet: Crafting a Sermon of Authority* (Valley Forge, PA: Judson Press, 1994); Marvin McMickle, *Living Water for Thirsty Souls: Unleashing the Power of Exegetical Preaching* (Valley Forge, PA: Judson Press, 2001); and E. K. Bailey and Warren W. Wiersbe, *Preaching in Black and White: What We Can Learn from Each Other* (Grand Rapids, MI: Zondervan, 2003).

12. Morna D. Hooker, *The Gospel according to St. Mark,* Black's New Testament Commentary (Peabody, MA: Hendrickson Publishers, 1991), 198.

13. Ibid.

14. Ibid.

15. See Thomas G. Long's *The Witness of Preaching* (Louisville, KY: Westminster John Knox Press, 1989).

16. Long, *The Witness of Preaching,* 66.

17. Walter Brueggemann, *1 Kings* (Atlanta: John Knox Press, 1983), 81–82. Brueggemann's specific quote—"whenever you read the words 'do not fear' in Scripture, they represent an injection of hope into an impossible situation"—was recited to me in a conversation I had with him at the Academy of Homiletics meeting in Atlanta, Georgia, on November 19, 2010. The quote is used with his permission.

18. Gerhard Ebeling has rightly noted that the primary phenomenon in the realm of understanding is not understanding *of* language but understanding *through* language. It is the word that opens up and mediates understanding, i.e., brings something to understanding. See Ebeling, *Word and Faith* (Philadelphia: Fortress Press, 1963), 318.

19. Charles Bartow, *God's Human Speech* (Grand Rapids: Wm. B. Eerdmans Publishing Co., 1997), 64.

20. Gardner C. Taylor, "A Holy Pursuit," in *Power in the Pulpit: How America's Most Effective Black Preachers Prepare Their Sermons,* ed. Cleophus J. LaRue (Louisville, KY: Westminster John Knox Press, 2002), 151.

21. Saint Augustine, *On Christian Doctrine* (New York: Macmillan Publishers, 1958), 142.

22. F. J. Foakes Jackson and Kirsopp Lake, *The Acts of the Apostles,* vol. 4 (Grand Rapids: Baker Book House, 1979), 210–11.

23. Hans Conzelmann, *Acts of the Apostles*, Hermeneia (Philadelphia: Fortress Press, 1987), 138.

24. R. C. H. Lenski and William Barclay do a much better job of helping to paint the picture of the city of Athens. See Barclay, *The Acts of the Apostles*, Daily Study Bible Series (Philadelphia: Westminster Press, 1976), 129–30; and Lenski, *The Interpretation of the Acts of the Apostles* (Minneapolis: Augsburg Publishing House, 1934), 707–9.

25. Cleophus J. LaRue, "Why Bother?" in *The Folly of Preaching: Models and Methods*, ed. Michael P. Knowles (Grand Rapids: Wm. B. Eerdmans, 2007), 221–25.

26. Bruce A. Rosenberg, *Can These Bones Live? The Art of the American Folk Preacher* (New York: Oxford University Press, 1970), 4.

27. A comment made in a sermon preached before the members of the Academy of Homiletics at their annual meeting on December 5, 2010, in Washington DC.

CHAPTER 9: HOW DOES ONE GET BETTER AT THE FOOLISHNESS OF PREACHING?

1. Nancy Gibbs, "How Much Does the Preaching Matter?" *Time*, 17 September 2001, 55.

2. George A. Buttrick, *Jesus Came Preaching: Christian Preaching in the New Age* (New York: Charles Scribner's Sons, 1932), 175.

3. Paul Scherer, *For We Have This Treasure* (San Francisco: Harper & Bros., 1944), 53.

4. Gardner C. Taylor, *How Shall They Preach* (Elgin, IL: Progressive Baptist Publishing House, 1977), 57.

5. Scherer, *For We Have This Treasure*, 68.

6. Fred Craddock, *Preaching* (Nashville: Abingdon Press, 1985), 77.

7. Karl Barth, "The Need and Promise of Christian Preaching," in *The Word of God and the Word of Man* (Gloucester, MA: Peter Smith, 1978), 117.

8. Walter J. Burghardt, *Preaching: The Art and the Craft* (New York: Paulist Press, 1987), 67.

9. Ronald Osborn, *Folly of God: The Rise of Christian Preaching* (St. Louis: Chalice Press, 1999), xiii.

10. Joseph R. Jeter and Ronald J. Allen, *One Gospel, Many Ears: Preaching for Different Listeners in a Congregation* (St. Louis: Chalice Press, 2002), 179–81.

11. This three-point outline is adapted from C. K. Barrett's *First Epistle to the Corinthians* (San Francisco: Harper & Row, 1968), 299.

12. Portions of this outline were taken from a sermon by Caesar Clark titled "A Misuse of the Morning," preached at the Missionary Baptist General Convention, Lubbock, Texas, 1978.

Index